WALK IN A RELAXED MANNER

Also by Joyce Rupp

Fresh Bread
Praying Our Goodbyes
The Star in My Heart
May I Have This Dance?
Little Pieces of Light
Dear Heart, Come Home
The Cup of Our Life
Your Sorrow Is My Sorrow
May I Walk You Home, with Joyce Hutchison
Prayers to Sophia
Out of the Ordinary
Inviting God In
The Cosmic Dance
Rest Your Dreams on a Little Twig
The Circle of Life, with Macrina Wiederkehr

WALK IN A RELAXED MANNER

LIFE LESSONS FROM THE CAMINO

JOYCE RUPP

ORBIS BOOKS
Maryknoll, New York 10545

Founded in 1970, Orbis Books endeavors to publish works that enlighten the mind, nourish the spirit, and challenge the conscience. The publishing arm of the Maryknoll Fathers and Brothers, Orbis seeks to explore the global dimensions of the Christian faith and mission, to invite dialogue with diverse cultures and religious traditions, and to serve the cause of reconciliation and peace. The books published reflect the views of their authors and do not represent the official position of the Maryknoll Society. To learn more about Maryknoll and Orbis Books, please visit our website at www.maryknoll.org.

Manufactured in the United States of America.
Design: Roberta Savage; Map: Ponie Sheehan

Library of Congress Cataloging-in-Publication Data

Rupp, Joyce.
  Walk in a relaxed manner : life lessons from the Camino / Joyce Rupp.
     p. cm.
  Includes bibliographical references.
  ISBN-13: 978-1-57075-616-0 (pbk.)
  1. Christian pilgrims and pilgrimages—Spain—Santiago de Compostela. 2. Rupp, Joyce—Travel—Spain, Northern. 3. Spain, Northern—Description and travel. 4. Christian life—Catholic authors. I. Title.
  BX2321.S3R87 2005
  263'.0424611—dc22
                                        2005009140

With much gratitude, I dedicate this book

to

Fr. Tom Pfeffer

soul friend

and

beloved walking companion

CONTENTS

Acknowledgments   8

Map   10

Along the Way   12

The Pilgrim Prayer   15

Introduction   17

Life Lessons

1. Allow the Historical Route to Empower You   25
2. Become a Pilgrim   33
3. Go Prepared   42
4. Walk in a Relaxed Manner   51
5. Let Go   59
6. Remember: Life Is a Great Adventure   68
7. Live in the Now   79
8. Be Attentive to Your Body   88
9. Acknowledge the Kindness of Strangers   96
10. Don't Let Difficulties Deter You   106
11. Embrace Beauty   116
12. Experience Homelessness   126
13. Return a Positive for a Negative   135
14. Keep a Strong Network of Prayer   145

15. Look for Unannounced Angels   153

16. Deal with Disappointments   161

17. Savor Solitude   170

18. Have a Sense of Humor   181

19. Trust in the Divine Companion   190

20. Let Yourself Be Humbled by Weakness   199

21. Enjoy Existential Friendships   208

22. Travel Lightly   218

23. Match Your Pace to Your Walking Partner   227

24. Enter into the Hum of Humanity   237

25. Pause to Reflect   245

After the Camino   253

Notes   258

Songs   259

*Sources Related to Pilgrimage and the Camino
de Santiago de Compostela*   263

ACKNOWLEDGMENTS

One of the lessons I relearned in walking the Camino is that our lives are constantly influenced and shaped by others. As I look back I am amazed by the number of people who blessed my time on the road to Santiago and contributed to the journey of writing this book:

Austin Repath gifted me with my first awareness of the Camino.

Bernard Thorne, O.S.M., shared walking tips and inadvertently gave me the title for this book.

Our friend Rev. Kevin Cameron surprised us with the gift of our pilgrim staffs and Bro. David Andrews used his hard earned frequent flight miles to give us tickets to Spain.

Linda Leedberg, Stan Caldwell, Sue Hodson, Maureen Chernick, Linda Garces, and Martilda Cudlipp gave essential help by sharing their Camino knowledge and experience.

Peg Madigan in Truro, Nova Scotia, and Joyce Mary Freyer, O.S.M., in Dorking, England, provided quiet places to write parts of this book.

Jennifer Sullivan and the community at Shantivanum Retreat center in Easton, Kansas, offered prayerful hospitality while Tom Pfeffer and I made our initial spiritual preparations in a retreat.

Beaverdale Back Country never tired of our endless questions about boots, raingear, and backpacks.

Charlotte Huetteman, O.S.M., hosted "prayer and party" celebrations at Emmaus House where friends and colleagues gathered to cheer us on and welcome us home.

Macrina Wiederkehr, O.S.B., wrote a special Camino blessing for us.

The St. James Confraternity in London, a central source for guidebooks and information on the Camino, was a priceless resource.

Those we met in Spain blessed us—marvelous pilgrims who encouraged us daily with their friendship and support, hospitable directors and volunteers who staffed the refugios each evening, and the residents of northern Spain who welcomed us and gave gracious advice.

Friends, family, Servite community members, and colleagues prayed for and with us each day.

Carola Broderick, B.V.M., Linda Caldwell, Jon Hrabe, and Rev. Ed Pfeffer reviewed my manuscript and helped immeasurably to shape it into something readable.

Michael Leach, Catherine Costello, Doris Goodnough, Mary Ann Ferrara, and Roberta Savage from Orbis Books used their valuable skills to get this book into your hands.

My deepest gratitude to everyone who walked with me in spirit during my astounding pilgrimage.

FRANCE

BAY OF BISCAY

ST. JEAN-PIED-DE-PORT

PUERTO DEL SOMPORT

Zubiri

Roncesvalles

Pamplona

Trinidad de Arre

Cizur Menor

Monreal

Estella

Jaca

Villatuerta

Puente

de Monjardín

la Reina

Sangüesa

Puente La

Reina de Jaca

NAVARRA

HUESCA

BURGOS

Santo Domingo

de la Calzada

Atapuerca

Tosantos

Logroño

Hontanas

Grañón

Azofra

Ventosa

Burgos

San Juan

de Ortega

LA RIOJA

ZARAGOZA

Boadilla

del Camino

PALENCIA

SPAIN

ALONG THE WAY

Before I left for the pilgrimage my co-author and friend of over thirty years sent me a blessing for the journey. I taped it inside the back page of my journal so its strength and courage would be with me every step of the way to Santiago. Little did I know how much her words would touch the life lessons I experienced on the Camino. Her words became increasingly meaningful to me as the weeks went by. I'll always be grateful for them.

May flowers spring up where your feet touch the earth.
May the feet that walked before you bless your every step.
May the weather that's important be the weather of your heart.
May all of your intentions find their way into the heart of God.
May your prayers be like flowers strewn for other pilgrims.
May your heart find meaning in unexpected events.
May friends who are praying for you carry you along the way.
May friends who are praying for you be carried in your heart.
May the circle of life encircle you along the way.
May the broken world ride on your shoulders.
May you carry your joy and your grief in the backpack of your soul.
May you remember all the circles of prayer throughout the world.
                                        Macrina Wiederkehr

We arrived in Madrid on September 4th and went on to Roncesvalles where we stayed overnight at a youth hostel that evening. We began walking the next day. During the ensuing weeks we found housing in one of the following cities, towns, or villages. Day 2 was our first full day of walking. After we arrived in Santiago we went on to Finisterre by the sea for five days of rest. We returned again to Santiago on the 18th and flew from Madrid to Iowa on October 20th.

Day 1	Roncesvalles
Day 2	Zubiri
Day 3	Trinidad de Arre
Day 4	Cizur Menor
Day 5	Puente la Reina
Day 6	Estella
Day 7	Villamayor de Monjardín
Day 8	Logroño
Day 9	Ventosa
Day 10	Azofra
Day 11	Grañón
Day 12	Tosantos
Day 13	Atapuerca
Day 14	Burgos
Day 15	Burgos
Day 16	Hontanas
Day 17	Boadilla del Camino
Day 18	Villalcázar de Sirga
Day 19	Ledigos
Day 20	Sahagún
Day 21	El Burgo Ranero
Day 22	León
Day 23	Astorga
Day 24	Rabanal del Camino
Day 25	El Acebo
Day 26	Ponferrada
Day 27	Villafranca del Bierzo
Day 28	Ruitelán
Day 29	O Cebreiro
Day 30	Triacastela
Day 31	Sarria
Day 32	Portomarín
Day 33	Eirexe
Day 34	Coto
Day 35	Arzúa
Day 36	Arca
Day 37	Santiago

THE PILGRIM PRAYER

Guardian of my soul,

guide me on my way this day.

Keep me safe from harm.

Deepen my relationship with you,

your Earth, and all your family.

Strengthen your love within me

that I may be a presence of your peace

in our world.

AMEN.

—Tom Pfeffer & Joyce Rupp

INTRODUCTION

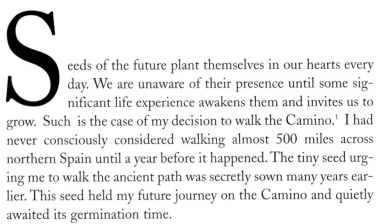

Seeds of the future plant themselves in our hearts every day. We are unaware of their presence until some significant life experience awakens them and invites us to grow. Such is the case of my decision to walk the Camino.[1] I had never consciously considered walking almost 500 miles across northern Spain until a year before it happened. The tiny seed urging me to walk the ancient path was secretly sown many years earlier. This seed held my future journey on the Camino and quietly awaited its germination time.

I was giving a retreat in Canada when I met Austin Repath. He had returned earlier that year from walking the Camino and told me about his pilgrimage to the tomb of St. James the Apostle in Santiago de Compostela. I was curious, especially when he said his experience was "life changing." Still, it was not enough to convince me I ought to do anything that challenging and lengthy. It seemed like a wonderful thing for *someone else* to do. So the seed of that amazing pilgrimage went into an extended fallow time.

Almost nine years after that Canadian retreat the kernel of the Camino began to sprout. Even now I cannot say exactly what it was that tickled the seed awake. It might have been when a friend discovered Shirley MacLaine's *The Camino*. MacLaine's experience intrigued me but I wondered if I could actually walk that long trek with its many insecurities and discomforts.

The seed of the Camino didn't really stir into life until my sixtieth birthday in the coming year loomed before me. I had this strong sense that walking the Camino was probably the best thing I could do for my own growth. I always said when I turned sixty I wanted to take a load of books and hide out for six months at some oceanside getaway and bask in solitude and silence. Tucked in my memory, however, was something C. G. Jung wrote, about adults in the second half of their life needing to allow their undeveloped self room to emerge and grow.

Six months of oceanside vegging out would only deepen my preference for introversion and seclusion. What I really needed was to "get out there in the world" and become immersed in something totally opposite, something definitely stretching that demanded my full participation. With these thoughts surfacing, the seed of the Camino stirred in its quiet home, sent out its first roots, and turned toward growth.

One day I mentioned the possibility of going on the Camino to my friend Tom Pfeffer. For over a year we had walked two or three miles several times a week on a bike trail by the Des Moines River. I asked Tom if he would like to join me on the pilgrimage. He was a dear friend of twenty years, the semiretired pastor of my parish, and I needed someone I could trust to be with me in what promised to be a giant undertaking. Tom was enthused at the prospect and gave me an eager, positive response. I was elated. Suddenly the journey seemed more doable.

After a year of planning and preparation, and months of training, we flew overnight from the United States to Madrid on September 3, 2003. From the airport we went by subway to the bus station where we waited for several hours before we took the five-hour ride to Pamplona. We then took a taxi, the only transportation at night available from Pamplona to the tiny village of Roncesvalles. This quaint village nestles high in the Pyrenees mountains, five miles from the French border. The next day, on the edge of that charming village enshrouded with morning mist and light rain, we first put our feet on the historical pilgrim route that took us all the way across Spain to where the cathedral of St.

James is located in the western city of Santiago. Thus began a great thirty-six-day walk that ended on October 10th and changed our inner lives profoundly.

Neither Tom nor I ever imagined we would learn so many spiritual lessons as we walked those hundreds of miles through the beautiful, diverse landscape of northern Spain. The journey became a transformative adventure, full of rich teachings. Each day we discovered something that added to our growth. Some of our lessons were new. Others were ones we had forgotten and needed to have restored to our consciousness.

WHEN THE SEED OF WALKING the Camino awakened in me, I hoped it would bear the fruit of spiritual growth. This definitely happened but when I returned home I wanted to hug this wonderful harvest to myself and limit my sharing of it. As a writer, I continually divulged my inner stirrings and insights. I thought, "This time, this experience will be *just for me*. The pilgrimage is going to be *mine*."

This desire was strong from the very beginning. I told few people about my preparations for the Camino. I determined that only family, several of my religious community members, and some close friends and colleagues were going to know. No shouting it "to the world." I also decided to limit emails from Spain to five or six people, to assure them from week to week that I was okay.

I had the whole thing planned for the fewest possible intrusions into my private life. Little did I know that each email I sent to the leader of my religious community was forwarded to all the members. When I learned this on returning, I did not change my plans for keeping the journey to myself. If anything, I increased this resolve. Yet, almost everyone who knew about the amazing journey asked me if I was going to write about it. Even though I kept a journal on the Camino and wrote in it daily, I easily responded: "No, this one is *just for me*."

People continued to raise the question. In my struggle over the issue, I spoke about it with Tom who seemed much more open than I was. He took great delight in telling others about the journey. Upon returning home, he responded enthusiastically to requests for conversations, even offering presentations about the pilgrimage. Being an extrovert, Tom totally enjoyed these opportunities to talk about his Camino experience with anyone who would listen. Not so for me. I kept trying to hug the pilgrimage to myself but the hope for privacy continued to unravel.

One day I met with three other women in my community with whom I share kinship. I told them about the struggle of not wanting to disclose my inner awakenings and life lessons of the Camino to the larger world. They understood and assured me I had every right to keep them to myself. That gathering ended at 1:00 p.m. At exactly 5:30 p.m. the same day I sat down to read an article by Doris Lora. The opening paragraph referred to mythologist Joseph Campbell, whose teachings I greatly admire. The author noted Campbell's description of the mythic hero as someone who ends a journey with one of two kinds of heroic acts:

> *A physical act in which the individual gives his or her life in sacrifice for others, or a spiritual act, in which the hero returns to share an extraordinary experience, and thus deeply benefits the community.*

Another seed suddenly sprouted—the beginnings of this book. As soon as I read that statement of Campbell's, I closed the magazine, jumped up and exclaimed to God: "Okay, okay! I get it! I get it!" There it was—the answer to my indecision. Finding this article was just too synchronistic and close to my struggle for me not to accept the call to leave my little niche of privacy. Finally I understood and accepted that the Camino journey was not just for me. I was the one returning from *"an extraordinary experience"* meant to be shared. My hope-filled intention would be to do so in order *"to deeply benefit the community."* [2]

Since that graced moment, I have been energized in my desire to present the life lessons of the Camino in a way that can invite you, the reader, into my experience of growth. What I did not realize is that in gathering and writing about these lessons, they have become even more real and alive for me. Gifts given away come back to greet us with their goodness.

Every significant journey changes us in some way. We are hardly ever aware of this while we are in the midst of it. We may have hints of these changes but it is only later, in looking back, that we gasp in amazement at what was being formed and shaped in our lives. Only then do we recognize how a new attitude, a stronger dedication, and a fuller passion stretched us into the fullness of life. Then we are able to identify the journey's ability to propel us into unexpected growth.

Unfortunately, our significant journeys can also alter us in negative ways we do not want. Sometimes we end up with greater disillusionment, deeper dissatisfaction, unending restlessness, frustrating confusion, or brittle patterns of disturbing anger and hostility. So much of what we learn from our noteworthy journeys depends on what we experience and how we go about responding.

Walking so many miles across northern Spain is a tough undertaking. Anyone who attempts this journey attests to its challenging and difficult aspects. There were certainly days when I was grouchy and discontented and times I felt my exhausted feet and aching back would fail me before I reached the day's destination. In numerous situations I wished I was back home in my cushy little bed. It is easy to make the difficulties and challenges the major focus of the Camino but the pilgrimage is about much more than these hard things.

There were scores of joyful times, kinship with others, daily adventures, endless beauty, and periods of great peace and tranquility. Each dimension of the Camino was a part of the growth process. Every step on the path opened insight and awareness and helped me to view my life more clearly. As I walked the many miles of the Camino, it led me to see how I get caught up in the cultural rush and hurry, the push and pull of calendars and never-enough-time. The Camino helped me look at the pressure of expectations and the strain of demands that I, and others, place upon myself. I am still in awe of the lessons the Camino provided.

The journey across Spain affected me more deeply than I imagined or hoped it would when I was walking it. Ironically, one day as Tom and I neared the end of our pilgrimage to Santiago we mused about whether or not we had grown. We decided the Camino had not changed us all that much, certainly not like others who described it as being "life changing." We agreed that probably some of our values and beliefs might have deepened a bit but nothing seemed "life changing" for us. What we did not realize, of course, was that we were still living the experience. We were too close for the lessons to be clear enough for us to perceive and fully understand.

I smile now as I recall that conversation. Little did I know that with every step I took on my walk toward Santiago, a huge change was unfolding in how I "did my life." Tom and I both began to understand and appreciate the richness of our journey when we were able to spend five days at the enchanted seaside village of Finisterre after we completed our walk to Santiago. As we reflected and shared what the pilgrimage had offered us for our inner growth, we started to glimpse the life lessons of the Camino.

It was not until we returned home that layer upon layer kept being peeled back. Underneath all the layers was one major truth for me: I had to let go of trying to control and have everything go the way I wanted it to go. I needed to look at *how* I did my life, not so much *what* I did with my life. The Camino reminded me that life is always going to have both ups and downs. I need to accept this as a natural process of growth and stop trying so hard to make it go my way.

Most of all, walking the Camino called me to allow daily life to be the pilgrimage and the adventure it truly is. As I slowed my pace on the Camino, I realized I had to slow down inside, stop being so intense, enjoy life more. I felt called to halt the constant push to be productive. The Camino showed me how much more I have yet to perceive and absorb in this regard. I will have to walk many more miles of life before this truth infiltrates and affects my life totally but the pilgrimage to Santiago greatly heightened my awareness of this essential ingredient.

I still do not fully recognize all of the life lessons nor totally comprehend my responses while walking the Camino. However, I trust that, just as with a night dream, if I am patient and spend reflective time with the pieces of my journey, these sources of significant change will become clearer. I offer you now these lessons that came from walking the ancient path of the Camino de Santiago de Compostela.

My desire in sharing these treasures with you is to have the teachings stir up fresh enthusiasm and hope for your life as they have done for mine. You may never have the opportunity to walk across the ancient path to Santiago but you will always have the opportunity to stretch and grow spiritually on your own path of life. May these lessons of the Camino that came to me one autumn in Spain plant a seed of growth in your own heart as you walk your daily pilgrimage of life.

1
ALLOW THE HISTORICAL ROUTE TO EMPOWER YOU

Walking, I am listening to a deeper way.
Suddenly all my ancestors are behind me.
Be still, they say. Watch and listen.

—*Linda Hogan*

Imagine walking on a path where millions of feet from other lands and cultures have previously walked, feet that have trod hundreds of miles to reach a sacred site. Think of what it would be like to have that same path and those same stones beneath your feet as you, too, walk for many weeks to reach the same destination. This is what it is like to be on the Camino de Santiago de Compostela.[3] It is a journey filled with spiritual connectedness and communal resonance.

This particular Camino is a revered walk to the cathedral of St. James in the city of Santiago in northern Spain where, according to legend, the bones of St. James the apostle were brought to rest. This pilgrimage is ancient. Some sources say it developed in the ninth century. Historical records definitely confirm the Camino as a popular pilgrim route by the beginning of the tenth century. I was amazed to learn that up to a million people walked the Camino during the Middle Ages. Currently, as many as 1,000 set out each day during the busy summer months. When these pilgrims complete their walk to Santiago they receive certificates at the pilgrim office near the cathedral of St. James. These certificates are signed and serve to authenticate the pilgrimage.

One aspect that attracted me was the spiritual energy I thought the old route held because of the many people who walked it before me. The endpoint of Santiago was not what primarily drew me to go on the Camino, although the cathedral of St. James is one of the most visited sacred Christian sites of the world.

People of varied religions and no religion visit the cathedral in order to experience the sense of something larger, fuller, and more profound than what is usually encountered in day to day living.

EACH SACRED SITE has spiritual energy for those who deliberately visit it. Not only is the spirit of the one who is honored present at that site. The good intentions and prayers of untold pilgrims add to the source of energy found there. What makes the Camino so special is that this source of renewal is present, not just at the destination point of Santiago, but all along the road one travels to reach the sacred site.

The spirit that pilgrims of olden years have left on the Camino is a spiritual vigor available for each pilgrim who walks it. The road to Santiago holds many kinds of ancestral power, including that of adventure, generosity, faith, purpose, companionship, trust, and courage. This energy can be missed, of course, if one is not open or aware but I think it is difficult to miss. Even those who set out on the Camino without any spiritual intention experience moments of awakening on this path. With each step toward Santiago, the spirit of past pilgrims who walked, sang, and prayed their way to the tomb of St. James fills the modern pilgrim with an unspoken grace, gifting each one with what he or she most needs.

As with numerous other pilgrims on the Camino, Tom and I experienced the spiritual potency of the Camino in the walking of it, rather than in reaching its destination. Initially, we thought *getting to Santiago* was the purpose of our walk. We soon discovered it was in making our way to the cathedral that we were to receive spiritual empowerment and renewed enthusiasm. Our life lessons unfolded among the numerous ups and downs the Camino provides. In the movement of each day, on the very same roads, paths, and streets other pilgrims had walked for centuries, we rediscovered a sense of the sacred. It was there we deepened our knowledge of how to walk through life in a relaxed manner. It was there we developed a pilgrim spirit.

The Camino's energy also comes through historical architecture. One is easily awed by the early Roman bridges that still span the rivers of towns and cities, the original Roman roads taking one forward toward Santiago, and the towering cathedrals and strongly built churches that continue to grace the Camino's path. It is over, through, within, and beyond many such historical markers that every pilgrim passes. In doing so, each traveler touches the vibrant energy of the journey, knowing those who made the pilgrimage in times past also experienced these same historical sights.

I sensed the Camino's energy immediately. With my initial steps, I felt an immense oneness with the countless number of pilgrims who previously traveled it. A flood of gratitude and joy moved through me. I knew it was holy ground. The spiritual ancestors of the way to Santiago had wanted to do this as much as I did. What had they experienced? What had they felt and seen? I couldn't wait to find out for myself. I wanted to walk the Camino with as much heart, as much grace, as much richness of spiritual experience as others did before me. My heart was high with hope as I set out, ready to receive the power each part of the path bestowed.

I noted in my journal the first day when we paused in a grassy area filled with tiny purple crocus-like flowers:

> *We have stopped at Viscarret, a small village, to rest. The walk here was very hilly and quite strenuous but also magnificent in views. Wonderful wildflowers: rose, lavender, and many I do not know. Such a surprise to find these blooming in September . . . We walked this first day from Roncesvalles into a magnificent forest with fresh, fragrant pine. A grace-filled walk. Already I have felt the energy and power of all those who have walked the Camino before me.*

Because of this keen awareness of the route's energy, a few days after Tom and I began walking on the sacred way to Santiago, we added two lines to a song by Jan Novotka that we sang daily. Every time we sang this song I was drawn anew to the ancestry of the historical route, feeling a joyful union with all who had been there before me:

> In the name of all that is we come together,
> *In the name of the pilgrims on the way,*
> *In the name of the people who have walked this path,*
> In the name of all that is, we come.[4]

We came in the name of countless people who had started out as we did. They gave vitality to the path by their presence. Each pilgrim today adds to that energy of pilgrimage. It makes no difference where one starts. Some begin their walk from the revered centers of Rome or Lourdes. Others originate from within their home countries, such as Italy, Belgium, France, Germany, or Holland, but almost all eventually meet up somewhere on the well-worn path that goes across northern Spain to the sacred site in Santiago. The most common starting point on the Camino is either the tiny village of St. Jean-Pied-de-Port on the French side of the Pyrenees or Roncesvalles on the Spanish side of the Pyrenees.

When Tom and I began walking the Camino at Roncesvalles, we followed the traditional pilgrim custom of wearing a scallop shell, another sign of union with the ancient pilgrim energy. The shell tells everyone that the traveler wearing it is on pilgrimage. There are numerous explanations offered for wearing the shell. One popular legend has it that when St. James's followers carried his coffin to land from the boat they were traveling in, they interrupted and surprised a wedding party on the shore. A horse spooked and bolted into the sea. Both the groom and the horse he was riding were presumed to have drowned. A miracle is attributed to St. James because the groom and the horse both survived the consuming waters. They came up out of the sea and strode triumphantly to the shore, with many scallop shells attached to the tangles of seaweed clinging to horse and rider. Thus the shell became a key symbol for those who journey to the cathedral of St. James.

Other legends are also connected with this ancient pilgrimage. I was elated when I learned this historical route is also called *La Via Láctea* (The Milky Way) because the direction of the path moves under this galaxy. A similar name given to it is Compostela, from two Latin words meaning "field of stars." Legend describes a shepherd, or a hermit, hearing some ethereal music and following the stars to a field where he discovered the remains of St. James's body. (On the sixth day of our walk, I was startled when we met an older Japanese pilgrim who told us his last name actually meant "field of stars." This unusual name was what drew him to walk the Camino.)

The dynamism of the stars, as well as the energy of past pilgrims, the historical sites, and the path itself, called to me as I walked on the Camino. I have long loved a star-filled sky. Standing out under the stars has always been a time of feeling connected to mystery and wonder. The prospect of walking for six weeks under this luminous sky-path intrigued and fascinated me.

However, I never saw the stars in the first weeks of the Camino. Each night I fell into bed exhausted, falling asleep before it was dark enough to view the stars clearly. It was not until we arose and walked in the predawn that I actually experienced this *La Via Láctea* energy. During a week when the sun was scorching hot we found that walking for a few hours in the cool shade of the night made it worth getting up before dawn. We used our small flashlights to guide our footsteps so we would not step into holes or trip on stones in the darkness.

There were several mornings when the waning moon sent out enough light to walk without using flashlights. Those were also the days when the road was smooth and easy to walk. Then I was able to look up often to where the stars were gleaming as far as the eye could see. They filled my heart with a reverent stillness. In those hushed moments I never doubted the historical energy cradled on the Camino. It surged in my soul on those mornings and sang melodies of pure delight.

It was not only the stars that left their energy in my soul. It was the land, the stones, the trees. Many places my feet touched gave me a sense of connectedness with something old and deep. One rainy day in Galicia we passed by two enormous oak trees. As I paused to appreciate their size and beauty, a mix of love and joy stirred inside of me. I felt the greatest peace. That night I happened to mention those trees to a pilgrim from Holland. The local people had told her the two oaks were over a thousand years old.

The next morning as Tom and I were leaving Triacastela, a hosteler asked us if we knew about an old oak tree on the edge of town. He said it was right on our way and encouraged us to stop to visit the tree because it, too, was over a thousand years old. We went and found the ancient oak. It had a huge, hollow space near the bottom of the trunk large enough for me to fit inside. So I went and sat "inside" the old tree. It was very powerful to be within the body of that ancient oak. I tried to open my heart as fully as I could to receive the arboreal energy the tree held for all those years, a gift readily present for anyone who passed by on the pilgrim route.

THROUGHOUT MY TIME of walking the Camino, the ancestral vigor of the path never left me. It culminated thirty-seven days later when I stood in the entry of St. James Cathedral. Before me was a tall marble pillar filled with carvings depicting the Tree of Jesse, that symbolic scriptural history of the Jewish and Christian lineage of Jesus. It is a strong symbol of faith passed down through the years.

I stood in line with tourists and other pilgrims completing their journey. As I came forward to place my hand in the handprint near the bottom of the pillar, a ripple of strong emotion caught me. I was astonished at what I saw: the indentations in the marbled handprint were worn deep from the millions of pilgrims whose hands were placed there before mine.

That moment at the Camino's end verified the powerful energy of the holy route. As my hand rested in the handprint on the pillar, I knew I was forever united with the presence of every pilgrim along the ancient path I traveled. As I walked the Camino, the faith-filled energy of the ancestors' courageous endeavors was imprinted on my heart. This surge of love and faith had carried and empowered me with every footstep along the way.

EACH OF US HAS a camino, a road of life. This road allows us access to the spiritual richness of those who traveled before us and those who travel with us now. All loving persons we encounter leave a touch of their positive, growth-filled goodness. We can slip into this energy as easily as my hand slipped into the deeply indented print in the marble pillar of St. James Cathedral.

Whether our sources of spiritual energy traveled life's path long ago or are still on it today, these people of faith are our teachers and catalysts of inspiration. Like pilgrims on the road to Santiago, their goodness empowers us as we set out each day to face the unknown, the beautiful, the challenging, and the rewarding facets of our historical journey. This potent energy stirs in our dreams, permeates our tough decisions with wisdom, and infuses hope into every new beginning.

2

BECOME A PILGRIM

At its heart, the journey of each life
is a pilgrimage,
through unforeseen sacred places
that enlarge and enrich the soul.
                    —*John O'Donohue*

I t sounds so romantic: *become a pilgrim*. Before I walked the Camino, I read numerous stories about pilgrims of various religions who set out to walk toward a sacred center. Each pilgrimage told of experiencing hardship and deprivation while also discovering spiritual growth along the way. Every story sounded both exciting and rewarding. Once I began my own pilgrimage, however, I quickly learned it's one thing to read about being a pilgrim and quite another to actually become one.

It didn't take long to discover what being a pilgrim is really like. Our first night on the Camino revealed what the future days and weeks held. Tom and I agreed we would begin our walk at the tiny village of Roncesvalles in Spain, rather than at the usual St. Jean-Pied-de-Port at the foot of the Pyrenees in France, which involves a long, strenuous, uphill trek of eighteen miles the first day. Even though we trained for walking long distances, we thought this might weary us too much at the beginning of our pilgrimage. So we chose the next place, Roncesvalles, which is at the top of the mountain, about five miles beyond the French border.

When we arrived at Roncesvalles, we needed to look for a "refugio."[5] Refugios are located all along the route and provide pilgrims with simple housing for a small monetary fee or donation. Our pilgrim guidebook assured us there were adequate sleeping accommodations in Roncesvalles in a huge monastery able to house up to three hundred pilgrims. What we did not know is that this refugio closed at the end of August. We walked in September/October and soon learned that while this time of year allowed for fewer crowds on the road it also meant some of the usual services for pilgrims were not available.

Because of our lengthy travel time from Madrid to Roncesvalles, we did not get to our destination until 9:15 in the evening. We easily found the darkened monastery but could not locate its entry. We tried one of the two local inns and were told the monastery was closed and both of the inns were full. "Whoa!" I thought, "This is way too soon to become a pilgrim!" Tom and I looked at each other and silently asked, "Where will we find shelter for the night?" Just then, a kind woman who worked at the inn motioned us outside where she pointed to a youth hostel nearby. She assured us we could find a place to sleep there.

We walked the short distance to this large building whose dark wood made it seem even more dense in the evening shadows. Few lights were on in the village. We took a deep breath and walked into a scene that would repeat itself for thirty-six nights. Inside we saw several long rows of bunk beds where many pilgrims had already settled in for the night like children at a summer camp. At the entrance of this enormous room with a high arched ceiling of wooden beams, someone ushered us over to a small table where two women stood. We quickly learned they were Dutch volunteers in charge of the hostel. Later we would often laugh and refer to them as "the Mother Superiors" of our first refugio.

The volunteers asked us for our passports. I was momentarily confused. Why did we need our passports here? Neither Tom nor I seemed to understand. As one of the women saw our confusion, she held up a small folder. We both laughed, realizing they meant our *pilgrim passports,* also known in Spanish as *credenciales.* Our tiredness was definitely showing because we eagerly awaited the time when we would hold these pilgrim passports in our hands. They would be our identification as a pilgrim and would assure any refugio director we were credible pilgrims allowed to stay in the refugios. Since this was our starting point on the Camino, the two women then prepared our *credenciales*. When they handed them to us, Tom and I enthusiastically accepted them with gratitude and joy.

What happened next startled me. One of the Dutch women corrected us for laughing and talking out loud. I thought, "Imagine me, the quiet, silence-loving one, being corrected for not being silent!" I almost started laughing again. Next, we were told that silence was strictly kept in the refugio and that the door closed at 10:00 p.m. No one would be allowed in after that. Another awakening. We had not eaten since our lunch in Pamplona so we scurried to the only place available for food. We went to La Posada Inn at the other end of the village to have the first of many bocadillos—a dry baguette with a thin, and I mean thin, slice of ham, and a thin, and I mean thin, slice of cheese, but it was food, and, anyhow, we didn't have time to eat more.

I felt exhausted as we hurried back to the refugio. We arrived just in time to have the lights turned out as we began to unpack our backpacks. It was pitch black. With our tiny flashlights, we unpacked our sleeping bags, toothbrushes, and the basic essentials. A lot of our things were inside plastic bags to protect the contents from heavy rain. Consequently, I felt nervous as I tried not to make rustling noise while I found what I needed for the night. I was sure every pilgrim trying to sleep felt irritated with me. (I discovered on future nights and mornings of packing and unpacking that many pilgrims made this noise with their own plastic bags.)

When I located what I needed, I carefully tip-toed with my tiny flashlight through the darkness to a staircase where there was light below. As quietly as I could, I walked the unsteady stairs down to a toilet and shower area. Only three women were there as all the rest were snug in their bunk beds already. They each nodded to me in greeting but no one entered into conversation. After my shower in the basement, I made my way carefully back upstairs. Some of the pilgrims were already snoring. All I cared about was finding my bed without getting into trouble with the Mother Superiors. I scrunched down by my bunk and unzipped my sleeping bag. Tom's bunk was next to mine. As I put my weary body into my sleeping bag, I turned toward him and whispered: "My God, why am I here?"

The morning was a rude awakening. All the lights came on at 5:45 a.m. Pilgrims arose instantly and long lines headed to the basement toilet area. In spite of still being tired, I felt a great excitement. This was it! We were really going to start out on the Camino! I was amazed I slept as well as I had with all those strangers. As I lay there for quite a while trying to absorb the reality of my actually being where I was, I listened to the shuffling back and forth of other pilgrims busy with preparations for the day. Finally I got up and headed downstairs. Women crowded around the two sinks where they quickly washed their faces and brushed their teeth. Others waited in line to use one of the two toilets. Already I missed my comforts of home. Back upstairs, I longed for privacy as I dressed amid the other pilgrims.

While I got ready to leave the refugio, I realized how hungry I was. I started thinking about having a delicious, fortifying breakfast before we began our first day of walking. With this comforting thought, my attention turned to repacking the backpack. I soon found out this was going to be a daily challenge. Because the sleeping bag went in the bottom of the pack to balance the weight, I had to take everything out each night. It was like emptying out a chest of drawers every evening before bedtime only to have to replace all the items the next morning, in the exact same order. It took over an hour that first day to get everything back inside the pack so it had the balance it needed to carry well. (It took me weeks before I could do this in half an hour.)

I still had a small pile of things to stow away when I heard a woman's voice loudly announcing: "Everybody out! Doors close at 8:00!" It was 7:57 a.m. I looked at Tom and we both raised our eyebrows—Mother Superior again. Sure enough, at 8:00 sharp the lights were turned off. They escorted us out the door and locked it behind us. Another surprise awaited us: it was raining. That meant trying to find some shelter by the front door as we dug into our backpacks to get our raingear to put over our other clothes. We then found coffee at one of the two inns. All they had for food were a few tiny packaged muffins. So much for a hearty meal to begin our first long day of walking. That morning was the beginning of daily longing for the food I knew back home.

I wrote in my journal later that day:

> *We started in the rain about 8:30. It was 10:30 when we stopped at a corner market and bought fresh fruit, cheese, and bread. We went on to walk 13 or 14 miles that first day. It was more than we thought we would walk but there were no refugios until then. The whole day's walk was filled with a beauty that energized us and gave us a desire to walk onward. Mountains close up and mountains in the distance, trees of all kinds and the flowers . . . the most beautiful ones were in the last half day of our walk, a little meadow of them and along the trail. The last 3 miles were really tough to walk, though. Muddy, cow manure all over, gullies full of rocks. A man ahead of us slipped and fell, not hurt. We are so grateful for our pilgrim walking staffs that Kevin gave us. To think we were not even going to bring any with us. My calves ache and the bottoms of my feet are sore from walking all day on stones, stones, stones—not the smooth asphalt we've been used to in Iowa.*

Along with the sense of wonder and amazement to actually be "walking the Camino" that first day, I was also aware that being a pilgrim did not mean it was going to be an easy journey. The days would hold much beauty but they would also be demanding. That much was clear to me.

On the third day of our journey, I was talking on and on about the tough conditions when I heard Jana[6] from Holland say:

"Pilgrims accept what is given to them." Hers was a message I needed to hear. She called me to be grateful for each piece of food I ate, each bed I slept in, and each person who treated me kindly along the way. Jana's comment reminded me to accept the conditions of being a pilgrim and to trust that the unknown path ahead would bring me what I needed for the journey.

There were continual reminders along the Camino of what being a pilgrim entailed. Each one pointed out a different aspect. On September 21st I read this note in the kitchen of the refugio at Villalcázar de Sirga. It was written in the four languages of English, Dutch, Spanish, and French:

> *Pilgrim, welcome. Make yourself at home. Take care of everything as it if were your own. Help to keep things clean and tidy. Think of those who will come after you and make them feel grateful. A pilgrim is a simple, sensitive, and very thankful person. See to it that you get your well-deserved rest. Your place should be vacant by half past eight in the morning. If you can, please make a monetary contribution. If you cannot pay, God bless you. Your memory and appreciation is sufficient for us. May St. James illuminate your way toward Compostela.*

Another one of these reminders presented itself along the route when we were walking to Nájera, eleven days after Roncesvalles. We rested in a pretty garden with benches alongside the Camino. Across from us, someone wrote a poem in Spanish in large letters on a concrete wall. "Pilgrim," it said, "what attracts you to the road?" Many stanzas followed, each giving possible motives for why one would walk the Camino. The poem ended by summarizing all the reasons with "only the One above knows."

No doubt a pilgrim on the way wrote the poem because it expressed a significant pilgrim truth: each one travels the path for his or her own reasons. Each person steps onto the Camino with a desire to walk it but is oftentimes uncertain as to why. The reason may be nebulous and unnameable for much of the journey.

Even if the motivation is explicit in the beginning, circumstances can easily alter it along the way.

To be a pilgrim is to be willing to live with the mystery of what will happen both interiorly and exteriorly as one walks day after day after day toward the destination of the sacred site. What happens inside cannot be planned or mapped out in the same way that the physical route is mapped. Becoming a pilgrim means there are no maps of the heart. One simply holds onto the hand of the Great Pilgrim and travels with hope that one day the spiritual benefits of the road will reveal themselves and be understood.

In being a pilgrim, the journey itself is of prime importance. We came across this truth in another quote, this time on a refugio wall in El Burgo Ranero. It said:

> *"Peregrina, (pilgrim) you do not walk the path, the path is YOU, your footsteps, these are the Camino."*

Tom and I had a long conversation about that quote and what we thought being a pilgrim meant. We knew beforehand that for us the Camino was not about the destination of Santiago nor about how many miles we walked. It was about what happened to us on the way, what took place in our hearts. The message we found on the refugio wall reinforced this truth for us.

Various books we read beforehand emphasized the value of being on the path, that even though the sacred site of Santiago was the endpoint of the journey, what really mattered was how we gave ourselves to each step along the way. The Camino taught us that the same is true for our pilgrimage through life. It is how we live, how we respond to what life brings us, that creates the difference in our spiritual journey. It is not waiting until death, the endpoint, before we become who we are meant to be. The process of being spiritually transformed into our truest selves happens all along the way.

At times I sensed I was becoming a pilgrim. The first of these moments was at the end of the second week when we stopped for a day and half rest in Burgos. We left the Camino path, found a hotel, enjoyed the pure luxury of a bathroom all to one's self, and indulged in the great food that the restaurants offered. This felt a little decadent after two weeks of living as simply as possible. I wrote in my journal that evening in Burgos:

> *Lamps and soft chairs. I've almost forgotten what a soft chair feels like. . . . At 3:30 when the shops reopened, we went to look for sandals and other items we needed to buy. Not back in our rooms until 7 p.m. Very weary of all the people, traffic, etc. Not used to it. While I like this hotel room and the privacy, it feels odd. I feel "out of sync." I am no longer a pilgrim. I want to be back on the path again. Can't believe I am writing this.*

I was learning that being a pilgrim is not something one easily takes on and off, like a piece of clothing. Something happens in the heart as one walks along the Camino without the comforts and securities of home. As a pilgrim, life gets simpler and the mind becomes clearer. The heart loses its hold on what is left behind and resonates more and more with the beauty of what is. Something secret and enticing keeps inviting the pilgrim to stay on the path, to go up another hill, to turn the next corner. In the rhythm of physical walking, the spirit gathers its own rhythm of adventure and harmony. Body and spirit befriend one another and, in doing so, are united in a new sense of oneness with something greater.

This pilgrim experience led me to leave the comforts of Burgos with an eagerness to be back on the path again. It took a day of walking, though, before I regained my inner stride. In the days after that, there were times when I desperately wanted to discard being "the pilgrim" but the call to continue on the route grew too strong and compelling for me to stop. I was en route on the Camino. I was a pilgrim living life more simply than I had ever done before.

The journey was walking me as I was walking it. I knew I would never be the same again.

3

GO PREPARED

Train wholeheartedly.
—*Pema Chodron*

Sometimes we overlook the most logical and necessary things when a great adventure beckons us. Reflecting back now I laugh at how needing to prepare for the Camino never occurred to me. I thought I would simply take a backpack and a pair of hiking books, get on a plane to Spain, and start out. If I had actually done that, I would probably not have lasted more than a few days. In fact, the second day, at Zubiri, I met a young woman from Perth who was totally exhausted from carrying a much too heavy backpack. She nursed badly blistered feet and had an exceedingly strained body from her two days of walking. She did just what I originally planned to do—set out with absolutely no preparation. Because she felt so beaten by the first days of walking, this Australian woman told me sadly she might not be able to go on.

I don't know if the young woman went ahead and continued on the Camino. What I do know is that I found preparing to walk the Camino absolutely vital. Tom recognized our need to pursue informative sources so we could learn what the journey required. Tom also insisted we get our bodies in shape for the long distances we would walk each day. I was not concerned about this because I walked a daily two miles or more for many years. It did not occur to me that I might need more stamina and durability for the long haul. When I decided to walk the Camino I never dreamed I would spend a good portion of my summer walking with a heavy backpack. Walking long distances wouldn't happen until I set foot on the Camino. Thank goodness Tom talked me into walking extensive mileage during the four months prior to our trip.

When I thought of going on the Camino, I focused more on the inward process, wanting to be spiritually prepared for the pilgrimage. In early March, Tom and I traveled to Shantivanum, a retreat center in eastern Kansas for some uninterrupted time to reflect on our motivations, hopes, concerns, and fears about the anticipated journey. Those days apart provided the initial spiritual preparation we needed. The days deepened our purpose and clarified our intentions. During the four-hour ride home we talked at length about what we pondered during our silent retreat time. We also composed the Camino prayer which we then prayed daily. Because of our reflection and prayer, we both returned from the retreat with a strong conviction that the journey was right for each of us.

Soon I discovered that Tom's approach and mine were both crucial for us to be adequately prepared. Without the mutuality of spiritual and physical preparation, we would not have had such an amazingly positive and growthful experience. Nothing could have fully prepared us for the challenge that the Camino conferred but our preparations provided a goodly amount of readiness for its hardships. Our preparations also continually enthused us about the coming pilgrimage. As we gradually grew stronger physically, we felt increasingly confident we would do well.

Tom and I read everything about the Camino we could find. At first, vital information was difficult to locate but once we discovered some good websites, the world of the Camino opened up. We read pilgrim accounts, learned crucial information, and ordered books to read such as *A Practical Guide for Pilgrims*. These sources gave us a better sense of the history, terrain, tribulations, and blessings of the path. We gleaned many helpful tips like the necessity of carrying enough water, what kind of socks and boots to wear, what to carry in our packs, how to avoid blisters, where refugios were located and how many beds they held. The beautiful descriptions of the varied landscapes of the historical route, plus the personal stories we read, whetted our eagerness for the trip.

We not only read, we also walked . . . and walked . . . and walked. In early May, we began with short distances of three to four miles at least four times a week. By mid May we upped the walks to five and six miles twice a week while keeping to the shorter ones on other days. On May 22nd we walked eight miles, our first one with our backpacks. The next day my legs and knees creaked and groaned from the lengthy trek along Saylorville Lake. My shoulder muscles were sore from my backpack, which felt like a bag of boulders attached to my body. I was thoroughly discouraged, wondering if I'd ever be able to really walk the Camino.

Never having carried a large backpack before, I didn't know I needed to adjust it to my body's height and size. Fortunately, a well-seasoned hiking friend happened to stop by several days later. He helped to fit the pack to my body, showing me straps I could move and regulate, as well as teaching me how to balance the weight within the pack. I breathed a sigh of relief once I learned those basic details. The next day I felt my pack settle more comfortably on my back and hips. After that, the preparation walks with my pack went more smoothly.

As we increased our daily walks up to a big fourteen-mile one, the mosquitoes hatched and swarms of them invaded our walking path. We used a lot of insect spray that summer. Iowa also grew more hot and humid. One day when we walked nine miles it was 92 degrees with strong winds of 40 mph as we crossed the open space of a wide meadow. We didn't give up, even though we were carrying 18-24 pounds in our packs that day to strengthen our backs. (We filled them with water jugs, books, and anything else that weighed a lot.) Part of the preparation was our intent to build up our endurance.

I was full of complaints. Most days, my feet were miserably hot, sweaty, and swollen in my hiking boots. I grumbled to Tom:

"Surely preparation doesn't have to be this tough." He kept reassuring me I'd be glad later on for those miserable days. I also felt frustrated and whined about how I hated taking so much time away from my precious work schedule. Because I would be away from my office for almost two months, I had promised myself a summer of writing. I longed for that space and was disappointed in how much of it was given to getting ready for the Camino instead. Tom continued to be a patient and steadfast listener. What a gift it was to have a walking companion who understood what I was experiencing and who reminded me daily that all the time spent in training would be worth it—and that I could do it.

In the midst of my grumbling and groaning, I went to visit my spiritual director. I told her of my strong resistance to the training time. At the end of our conference she smiled at me with her wise eyes and gave me a significant send-off: "Remember the preparation is as important as the journey itself." I didn't like her comment much. A little voice in me whimpered: "She should have said something more encouraging and hopeful." I was getting attached to my growling. I still felt my summer was a lost endeavor because I was not getting done what I wanted. In spite of that, when I went back to the long, daily walks, I tucked her comment in the back of my mind, hoping it might make sense one day.

There were some preparations that were fun. Besides the time-consuming physical training, we also talked to people who had walked the Camino. It was exhilarating to meet these seasoned pilgrims. They helped our preparation by giving us a firsthand account of their experiences, along with sharing good advice. We were surprised to meet several pilgrims from our own city of Des Moines. Both Tom and I marveled at Stan Caldwell and Linda Leedberg's enthusiasm, as well as their graciousness to us. They invited us for dinner and shared everything they could of their Camino experience, including the spiritual beauty they had found. Sue Hodson was another pilgrim who took time to meet with us at her home. Sue spoke about the presence of other pilgrims she met and how much she valued those encounters. Sue encouraged us to be open to other pilgrims who walked and to spend time with them. Soon after this, another friend put us in touch with a couple from Arizona who were close to our age. They gave us great advice on how to take care of ourselves, especially our feet.

Each day something called out: "Prepare!" While we walked, read, talked, and prayed, we also shopped for what we needed: raingear, sleeping bags, thin liner socks, etc. We copied maps out of books so we wouldn't have to carry the heavy books. I started drinking just one cup of coffee in the morning, knowing I'd be lucky to have even one cup before I started my walk each day on the Camino. I even tried to keep the shower water cooler as I read about those infamous cold showers in some refugios.

As the days drew closer to leaving for the Camino, I began to see how the time, energy, and effort put into the training I had resisted and questioned was going to help significantly on the journey. One thing was obvious: more than anything else, our preparations strengthened us. This was certainly true on a physical level. My feet and legs developed greater endurance and my back muscles carried my pack more easily. I grew increasingly confident that I was capable of the Camino's many miles. On an inner level, I was also strengthened. Praying the Camino prayer daily and constantly tending to my fears and concerns served to bolster my trust in the Holy One's guidance and care. Each week my heart held a firmer sense that there would be many spiritual benefits from the pilgrimage.

Something else I discovered from our training time was that there are often unforeseen blessings to accompany and balance the work which preparation requires. In the summer months when Tom and I walked endlessly in the heat, we encountered much beauty on the trails: verdant green foliage touched with drops of rain, twin fawns romping with a doe, bald eagles skimming over the river, countless wild flowers, and elegant, swaying prairie grasses.

The blessings included the good talks we had on our long training walks where we learned more about one another. Another gift was the experience of unity with other bikers and walkers on the trails, as well as an ongoing sense of accomplishment in what we had done for our training.

Preparing to walk the Camino taught me how necessary it is to remember the benefits and rewards of endless preparation in any aspect of life. When I am struggling to meet the deadlines in writing a book, I forget the pleasure of bringing the contents of a book together. Parents who are raising children to adulthood can miss the beauty and joy of these young ones as they nurture, care for, and discipline them. Students easily sidestep the marvelous things they learn as they face the pressure of grades and papers. Parish staffs lose sight of the possibilities of spiritual growth when they get mired in endless planning for formation programs and liturgical celebrations. Managers and organizers fail to notice the difference their hard work makes in the lives of their employees.

The lessons that came from the preparation time never seemed to end. Not until I was on the Camino did I understand my spiritual director's farewell comment to me. Without our concentrated preparations, I might not have recognized this truth. All those sweaty days of walking helped me see how essential it is to pay a price for the good things I want to come my way. Most of life's joys and pleasures do not come freely. Preparing for the Camino convinced me there are myriad and diverse costs which life demands in return for personal growth and satisfaction.

My prepilgrimage training not only strengthened me, it taught me about having to give up one good thing for the sake of another. I could not have everything I wanted without letting go of something. I had to forego my desire to write to give time to training. I had to disengage from one center of attention in order to give my wholehearted energy to another center of attention.

If anyone wants to accomplish something significant in work or personal life, it usually does not happen automatically. Choices have to be made. We must give ourselves to the necessary preparation for what we desire. In order to enter into what we hope for, we may need to allow ourselves to sacrifice something we enjoy or prefer to do. Most of us experience resistance to the price to be paid or else we refuse to give up one thing for the sake of another. We long for certain changes in our lives but are unwilling to do what it takes to make those changes happen. Something in us is unwilling to accept what is necessary for us to move into uncharted territory.

Yet, for certain changes to happen, preparation is crucial. The situations are many: studying for an advanced educational degree to attain a pay raise, pausing to exercise in order to stay healthy, giving time to extended conversation or social activities for the sake of developing a new friendship, taking time to read so as to be more informed and skilled, rising earlier in the morning to have quality meditation time, preparing for a return to good health as one recovers from an illness by receiving help from others. All these are forms of preparation leading to future satisfaction in a new venture but we must be willing to pay the price to realize these endeavors.

When I returned home from the Camino, I noticed how I tend to resist paying the price for what I want. I paid attention to my dislike for taking time to cook a meal but also my pleasure when friends came to my home for dinner. I saw how I derived much satisfaction from speaking to groups but fought the time it takes to prepare a talk and how I detested packing a suitcase but relished meeting people in my travels to new places. Carrying my heavy notebook computer was another price I resisted but I was grateful when I pulled it out of my bookbag and used it.

EACH LIFE OF OURS, no matter what our work or way of living, necessitates preparation for what we hope to attain in our endeavors. We cannot always see or know what the results of our efforts will be, nor can we initially understand how it might help our future experience. Preparation may require of us some unexpected time and energy. It might ask for additional study or reorganizing our daily schedule, or tossing out an activity we enjoy. This much I know: in the end, going prepared by doing the work required, by paying the price demanded, will make the new growth worth the effort. It certainly did this for me on the Camino.

My spiritual director was right. The preparation is definitely as important as the journey itself.

4

WALK IN A RELAXED MANNER

The simplicity of resting—
there is much profoundness in that.
— *Khandro Rinpoche*

51

The biggest lesson I learned on the Camino was that I needed to slow down. It was the most difficult thing to learn. It came to me, as did many of the other lessons, in a slowly awakened way. Had I been more alert during the summer preparation time when I felt harried and hurried, I might have been ready for this challenging teaching.

As it turned out, the lesson came in the early days after we started our walk in Spain. Tom and I both became increasingly tired and disgruntled with our pressured pace during the first week. It was ironic, there we were thousands of miles away from home and work, with seven weeks free from "have to dos" and "don't forgets." We had no lists to make, no phone calls to be returned, no mail to open, no meetings to attend, no requests to acknowledge, no deadlines. Nothing. What a grand opportunity to relax and be released from the pressure of *getting things done.*

Then why, we asked ourselves, were we hurrying and rushing to get to the next refugio? Why did we try to keep up with the other pilgrims who were zooming past us at express speeds? What urged us to accelerate our pace and count our miles so precisely? Why did we hesitate to give ourselves adequate time to rest? What was the source of this self-imposed pressure to keep moving faster, to hurry forward to each day's destination?

One major cause of our pushing onward was the need to find housing each night. Every day we started out earlier than some of the other pilgrims who stayed at the same refugio but they always caught up and passed us by later on because we walked more slowly. About mid-morning we would hear the clickety-click and the thumpety-thump of metal and wooden walking sticks behind us. Soon these pilgrims (mostly physically fit Europeans accustomed to hiking) would dash past us at incredible speeds. Pilgrim after pilgrim zipped by us on the path. When this happened, I got a sinking feeling Tom and I were the last ones on the road. A growing desire shoved me on to go faster, to enter the race with everyone else. It was obvious to me that we were definitely going to be *left behind* if we didn't *hurry up*. I pressed forward, causing Tom to reluctantly do the same.

Seeing all the other pilgrims hurrying along served as an anxiety raiser because it meant they would get to the refugios long before us and be able to claim a bed there. We soon understood there were only two or three refugios within the distance of the day's walk. In those places a limited amount of beds was available. Refugios did not take reservations so the early birds who arrived first would find a place to sleep that night and we late-comers would not.

Another reason for hurrying was a silently competitive voice inside me growing louder every day. Tom and I gave ourselves a set amount of time to get to Santiago. We figured we needed to walk an average of ten to twelve miles per day in order to arrive there in our allotted time. If we kept to this average mileage each day, we were confident of easily meeting our estimated goal.

I was okay with limiting our miles until the third night when we heard a sturdy German pilgrim announce he had walked thirty miles that day. I felt like a wimp by comparison. Then, when I saw others zooming along at high speeds which took them many more miles per day than us, a voice inside chided that we should do more. While Tom was more comfortable than I with walking slowly, he too picked up the pace. Who would believe a competitive spirit burned and thrived on a pilgrimage—but there it was.

BESIDES DEALING WITH this self-inflicted stress of comparison, the Camino also challenged me to accept my aging process. At sixty, I simply could not walk as quickly and nimbly as a twenty- or thirty-year-old. I needed to walk more slowly, rest regularly, and make sure my body received good care. Every day the Camino reminded me of my age. Quite honestly, I did not want to appear old, trudging along without the energy of the more youthful pilgrims. My ego wanted to keep up, make a good appearance, show them I could do it. (Another lesson! I took my ego with me, even on the Camino's sacred path.)

Gradually I accepted my diminishing energy. I learned to be at peace with it. I also grew more grateful because the deliberately measured pace helped me slow down inside, causing me to become more contemplative as I walked along. This did not happen the first week, however. During the first week our sense of urgency continued to grow. Each morning we made as early a start as possible. We packed our backpacks faster. If we stopped for mid-morning coffee, we didn't tarry long. When we met other pilgrims we cut our conversations short. When we paused to rest our feet, we kept the stop brief.

Our unspoken motto became: Push onward. Push forward. Push, push, push. Rush, rush, rush.

We soon discovered that the rushing and pushing caused us to lose our enjoyment of the walk itself. We left home in order to experience the freedom of *getting away from it all* but we simply took the tensions with us in new forms. The *place* of our stress changed but we had not changed. We continued to strain and groan under the desires and expectations of achievement and accomplishment—goals which our culture thrives on and implants in us almost from birth.

FINALLY, TOM AND I had a good talk and both agreed the stress of hurrying denied us our inner harmony and the spiritual adventure of the Camino. We decided to slow down. In order to do that we needed to change our attitude and behavior: no more rushing, competing, and worrying. We finally took to heart a significant message that arrived the day before we left for Spain. I received this wisdom in an email from Bernard Thorne, a Servite friar in Ireland. When I was with Bernard at a meeting in Portugal in July, I was astounded to discover he was headed for the Camino two days after the conference. I asked Bernard if he would email some advice to help Tom and me on our walk when he returned from his pilgrimage experience. Bernard promised to do so.

The day after Bernard returned I received a very short note from him saying he had little advice to offer except to tell me that during the first two weeks of his walking he "had a lot of blister trouble." He then went on to describe how he met an old man in one of the refugios during the second week. This old man looked at his blistered feet and advised: "Drink more water and walk in a relaxed manner." This bit of counsel made an immense difference for the rest of Bernard's pilgrimage. When he slowed down and drank more water his blisters left and, at the same time, his peace of mind and heart returned.

Walk in a relaxed manner. Much easier said than done. Tom and I were productive-oriented people, the kind you can count on to get things done. Both of us were in church ministry, which we gave ourselves to full-heartedly. (Fool-heartedly, too!) Tom was semiretired but still felt inundated with way *too much to do.* As for me, I continually faced stacks of unanswered mail, deadlines for retreat talks and writing, as well as numerous social commitments. The months before I left for Spain I felt constantly frazzled, try-ing to *get it all done* before I left for almost two months. I'd get one thing finished in the office and ten more items popped up, demanding my attention. This was nothing new. I experienced this pressured approach almost every day, like many other people I knew. These busy colleagues and friends all went through the same thing so I accepted pressing and hurrying as the *normal* way to live if one chose to be responsible, faithful, and successful.

This lifestyle does not work for a physically and spiritually healthy Camino, nor does it work for a truly healthy life anywhere. It leads to anxiety, distress, and discontent. I discovered during my days as a pilgrim that I could not be at peace unless I walked in a relaxed manner both internally and externally. I had to come to terms with why I felt a need to push, to rush, and always to give too much time to *getting somewhere and doing something*.

Was it due to religious and social expectations, the pressures of the job, or my own inherited sense of responsibility? After many days of walking on the Camino I decided it was a combination of all of those things and that it was definitely something I wanted to alter in my attitude and actions. I had to slow down inside, change the messages I gave myself about achievement and responsibility. Walking in a relaxed manner on the Camino was a great catalyst for that attitudinal adjustment.

Once Tom and I decided we wanted to pace ourselves differently, the days on the Camino gradually changed for us. We discovered that our outer action of slowing down our walking also influenced our inner tempo. We grew more peaceful and enjoyed our time with other pilgrims instead of envying their faster walking strides. The beauty of the Spanish countryside took on a deeper color and hue. Its people seemed to grow friendlier by the day. We worried less and were more at home with ourselves and one another.

The wisdom of the old man's advice to Bernard also helped us physically. Slowing down our pace proved to be much easier on our feet. They did not get as heated, which meant they were less likely to form blisters. Our legs felt less tired. We found we could actually walk our daily miles much easier than if we pressed at a quicker pace. The other blessing of going slower was that Tom's easily irritated ankle behaved itself once we stopped pushing so hard.

Another way we stopped hurrying was to take longer rest

periods as we made our way westward on the pilgrimage. We basically took three kinds of rests: little ten- to twenty-minute ones throughout the day, longer half-day ones when we ended our walking by 1:00 or 2:00 in the afternoon, and big ones of a whole day when we did not walk at all. We found, eventually, that the rests we enjoyed the most were the times when we walked around five hours and then stopped for the day. These half days provided a welcome relief from the usual hurrying we were tempted to do when we did not get to a refugio until 4:00 or 5:00 p.m. or later. Stopping early gave us adequate time to hand wash our clothes, take a shower and nap, buy provisions for the next day, stroll leisurely around the town to see any historical sites, study our guidebook, and make plans for the next day's walk. We tried to give ourselves one or two of these days a week and found that when we did so, there was a noticeable change in our spirits.

Walking in a relaxed manner is challenging. There was just too much "hurry" built up in us through the years to keep us from instantly changing our ways. Whenever we thought we were well established in our new attitude and behavior, one of us would want to go further than we originally agreed. At other times one of us would pick up the pace physically or start voicing concern about whether or not we'd find room at the next refugio. We had to constantly give our attention to going slowly in spirit as well as in body. It took effort to be present to the new approach we were birthing and growing as we walked. Tom and I reminded each other of this often by simply saying: "Don't forget: Relaxed manner!" or "Time to stop hoofing it!"

When I came back home from the Camino, I observed how rushing and hurrying and pushing are evident everywhere. Over-achievement, competition, comparison, addiction to work and duty, unreal expectations of needing to do more, the obsessive pursuit of having more—all these fall on us as heavy cultural and self-imposed burdens. When these attitudes and messages press in on us, they cause us to lose our harmony and self-satisfaction.

There is far too much hurry and worry in most lives. There never seems to be enough time to complete the daily chores of laundry, lawn care, meal preparations, phone calls, and paying bills, let alone the pressure of other accomplishments that people feel compelled to do. Parents with children involved in an over-abundance of activities, health care workers working double shifts, educators saddled with extracurricular tasks, managers with countless meetings, retired people with too much scheduled—these are some of the many people who need to walk in a relaxed manner, but who find their responsibilities and overextensions make it difficult to do.

Undoubtedly, it will take a lifetime for me to fully learn the lesson of walking in a relaxed manner. All too easily I am thrown off balance and lose my peaceful equilibrium. When this happens, I ask myself questions like these: Why am I allowing myself to be stressed? Who and what is most important in my life? What is my motivation for what I am doing? How is my ego influencing the pressure I feel? Am I being overly responsible or too competitive? If I died tomorrow, would what I am doing be of importance? These questions usually help me regain my balance.

I believe with all my heart that it is nigh impossible to walk in a relaxed manner externally unless I walk in a relaxed manner internally. I now know that if I change my attitude and approach to life, I will be encouraged to make decisions that help me slow down the rest of my life. The reverse is also true. If I slow down on the outside, internally I will also relax. I long to be able to say what author Thich Nhat Hanh said: "I am not running anymore; I have run all my life; now I am determined to stop and really live my life."

I still have a tendency to run but I am slowing down more often. I even walk slowly sometimes. Every day is a day to walk in a relaxed manner. I'm getting better at it.

5
LET GO

They say in old stories that you can't discover
new lands without losing sight of the shore
for a long time.

                                    —*Laurie Gough*

Some life lessons I learned on the Camino were not new. Walking the Camino reawakened their importance for my growth. This was certainly true regarding the lesson of letting go. This significant teaching revealed itself to me in the weeks before I left for Spain and it presented itself over and over on the pilgrimage. Although I am a risk taker, letting go has often been difficult for me. I can readily slip into wanting to grasp and hold onto the familiar and the comfortable.

The day we left for Spain I was especially mindful of what I was leaving behind and what I wanted to hold onto: the beauty and tranquility of personal space, a comfy bed, soft chairs, bookcases full of good reading, favorite music, a refrigerator and cupboards with healthy foods, a phone and computer readily available for contact with others. The more I thought about it, the more the desire for ease and comfort tugged at me. I longed to walk the Camino but hesitated to leave my nest of contentment to do so. I did not look forward to the prospect of spending every night for almost two months in a sleeping bag and having to share sleeping quarters with lots of snoring strangers.

The more I thought about what I was leaving behind, the more I was tempted away from my enthusiasm. I wrote in my journal the next day:

Yesterday before I left the house for the airport, I sat at my silent computer and prayed. I stood by the patio and looked out at the

trees and birds. I paused in the living room, by the flower garden,
and in all the places I enjoy. I realized I have to let go, to leave
behind, in order to go on to something new. As I looked at the
trees, I said to them: "You will be different when I return. All
your leaves will be shed. You will be barren again. Will I also be
different? How will I change? What will these seven weeks of
walking and walking do to me? How will it be to live a simple,
uncluttered life?" The answers are hidden from me. I only know
that I have to leave all this behind if I am to go forward.

Deep down, of course, I realized the necessity of letting go as
the only thing to do. Holding on too tightly to anyone or anything
only deprives oneself of growth. Clinging too tightly to something squeezes the life out of it. Hanging on for dear life for security's sake prevents one from what the future offers. I *did* want to
go forward. I *did* want to grow. So I walked out the door with
hope in my heart, knowing that *letting go* involved a price to pay.

It took just one day on the Camino to understand that I had
barely begun the process of letting go. Leaving my familiar place
at home was the easy part. Many other things required my acceptance. Some of them were unexpected little things, like thinking
every refugio would have the kind of silence I experienced my first
night on the Camino. There, at Roncesvalles, all the pilgrims
dutifully kept the silence required in the refugio. The second night
was a different story. Not only were there all kinds of conversation
and noise in the sleeping area before the customary 10:00 p.m.
silence, the racket continued long afterward. The noise made it
difficult to fall asleep and aggravated my longing for solitude and
quiet. The next morning the same chatty group of pilgrims arose
at 5:30 a.m., talking loudly, slamming doors and clomping around
in their hiking boots, seemingly with no thought for tired pilgrims
(like me) who were still trying to sleep.

After that experience I thought: "Wow, letting go is going to
be a daily challenge." It was. Grubby showers and bathrooms,
greasy food, refugios crammed with too many pilgrims in a small

space, reconciling my age and inability to walk as fast as younger pilgrims, and maneuvering through piles of cow manure on the paths—these kinds of challenges constantly presented themselves to me.

When I wrote in my journal, I described places that lifted me out of my comfort zone:

> *Another refugio was run by a middle-aged Spaniard who wanted to offer hospitality to pilgrims. The place was the absolutely worst, dirtiest place. A huge German shepherd sat by the entrance. Not far from this, a large old tin bowl partially filled with milk and pieces of food lay on a table outside the adobe hut. Another building and a small stable were nearby. A young woman with an apron appeared. Her clothes were torn and horribly dirty. She smiled and looked completely happy. I can't imagine staying there.*

I later learned of a pilgrim who did stay at that refugio. He slept on the dirt floor and felt quite content with the place.

A lot of my struggles with letting go related to my expectations. Having traveled overseas considerably I never looked upon myself as the "Ugly American" but on the Camino my initial responses to situations like that refugio indicated I was living up to that description. I expected public restrooms to be along the well-traveled route. There were none. I expected toilet and shower facilities in the refugios to be reasonably clean. Most were dirty. I expected each place to have communal prayer in the evenings or mornings. Only a few refugios did. I expected restaurants and stores to be open for my convenience. Instead, they honored siesta and opened on their own Spanish schedule. I even expected the sun to rise and set at the same time as it did back home when Spain's two hours of daylight savings time created darker mornings.

With some of these cultural differences, the challenge to let go was simply a matter of awareness and acceptance such as the silence in refugios or the time variation. Other situations like dirty restrooms remained a struggle for me throughout the entire Camino and humbled me with their ever present challenge to let go.

Some of my letting go issues were not of external things but of internal ones, like expectations and desires regarding myself. I expected to push my body into doing what I wanted but it refused to walk too fast or too far without pain. I expected my memory to serve me well but it left me in the lurch on several occasions, with difficult consequences. I expected to always be a model pilgrim of love and good humor but there were days when I was grumpy and irritable. I expected to not get sick if I took good care of myself but I got sick anyhow.

EVEN SENDING EMAILS home demanded some letting go. I had a tough time figuring out how to use the computer system in some internet cafés. The keyboards were different and while I was happy to be able to send a quick email to friends and family back home, I felt frustrated by the unfamiliarity and the time it took to write a short note. I grumbled about wanting a keyboard like the one in my office.

Many of my challenges to let go involved being willing to enter into another society and accept its differences. Adapting to another culture is absolutely essential if one is to walk the Camino with any degree of peacefulness. This adaptation to culture is true for any country where I have traveled. To expect that things will be like they are back home is to question why anyone would even bother to spend time outside one's own borders. I know this truth in my head, of course, and it fits in perfectly with my philosophy of life. However, I had to learn this lesson of being open to another culture all over again when I was on the Camino.

In walking the route to Santiago, I realized it is relatively easy for me to accept another country's customs and lifestyle—when I am rested and comfortable—but not when I am tired and in need of solace. Then I stop philosophizing and begin crabbing. One of my biggest challenges regarding the culture of Spain concerned the lateness of people's evening meal. The time would have been all right if I had been an ordinary tourist but I was a pilgrim, getting up early to walk miles and miles, and starved by day's end. Restaurants rarely opened before 8:30 p.m. and often not until 9:00. I knew about this custom before I arrived and I did not think it posed a problem. I presumed I could find fast food places or a small cafés for my meals. Alas, no fast food places existed and cafés and bars did not open until 7:30. Not until I walked fourteen miles with only a sandwich and a piece of fruit for lunch, did I understand the hardship this custom placed on me.

The Spanish custom of siesta also challenged me. Siesta time is important to the people in Spain and they hold tenaciously and wisely to this healthy feature. Almost all shops close by 1:00 or 2:00 p.m. and do not open again until 4:00 or later. There were many days when I arrived at a refugio voraciously hungry, looked around the village for a place to buy food but needed to wait until late afternoon before any store opened.

What a difference from our American pace of life when many drugstores and marts stay open twenty-four hours a day. Because most essentials are instantly available in the U.S., I wrongly assumed the same for Spain. This custom challenged my patience and required that I either adapt to the culture or else constantly complain because things were not *like back home*. It was time to let go.

My patience grew slowly and steadily, along with my acceptance of the culture's differences but just when I thought I let go, my patience grew thin again. This proved particularly true when we stayed a day to rest in the beautiful city of Burgos. Because we had been walking for several weeks by then, there were some small items we needed to buy or replenish such as suntan lotion, a small scissors, black thread, and socks. Tom also wanted to buy some sandals. I whined to Tom late that afternoon, "I am so tired. I thought we came to Burgos to rest from walking. We've walked miles around this city to many different stores to purchase the items we could have found in just one store in the U.S." Instead of enjoying the great variety of little shops, I slipped into the old pattern of hanging on tightly to *my culture* because of my weariness and desire to rest.

Letting go involved more than the daily basic comforts. Many things required constant relinquishment. Tom and I needed to let go of people: the further we walked on the Camino the more pilgrims we came to know and enjoy, and the more of them we had to say goodbye to as they traveled on ahead or were left behind. We had to change our notion that all pilgrims walk the Camino because of a spiritual motivation. Even the beauty of the landscape required letting go as we moved on to other regions. Refugios, too, called us to let go: when we found a clean, homey one we knew it was only for one evening. The Camino constantly told us, "Enjoy what you have now but do not hang on to it."

I noticed that the more I deliberately let go, the more peace of mind and heart I acquired. Things that were so important to me in the beginning of the Camino lost some significance as I learned the lesson of constantly letting go. Gradually, I became more satisfied with what was. Several entries in my journal point to this change:

> *Now there is a young German couple come out to the terrace to sit. After last night, men and women in the same bathroom and showers, the crammed bed conditions, I am almost at the pilgrim-point of saying: "Whatever I have for housing is okay." First, I wanted a bottom bunk bed, privacy in the showers and toilets, toilet paper. Now, five days later, I am glad to have a bed, a place to wash up, a place to go to the toilet. No paper, no soap, no privacy, mattresses like soft hammocks. Who cares? I have a place to sleep!* (Sept 10)

I am slowly getting into the pattern of these weeks ahead. Slowing down. Leaving my "regular life" behind, letting go of past and future expectations. There is one shower and toilet for all of us in this room. You can hear everyone's bathroom noises. In one corner there was a patch of ugly vomit that needed to be cleaned up when we first got here. Outside there's another shower and toilet for another room full of people. We both agree this is a good place. I laugh at this. How quickly something I would detest back home becomes something I rate as good here. Bunk beds are still close together but I am getting into the routine. Refugios just are. They provide shelter and this is what is vital. (Sept 12)

Amazing how my "needs" have deteriorated. First I wanted privacy, not general bedrooms. Then I wanted a bunk bed with a pillow. Now I am thrilled when I get a lower bunk, no matter what the condition of the mattress or pillow. Some beds have pillows, some even with pillow cases, many without. Some have soft coverings on the mattress, others have noisy plastic covers. Some are dirty, others are clean. Some bunk beds are very high and hard to get out of, especially when they don't have little ladders on the side. Others have so little space on the bottom bunk that you cannot sit up without hitting your head. (Sept 21)

This gradual letting go was no more apparent than in my pilgrim friend, Aileen. In the first days of getting to know her we were sitting at a table by an outdoor café, eating our lunch of bread and cheese. There were zillions of flies swarming around our food. Aileen kept swatting at them and complained, "How can you stand to eat your sandwich? These flies are horrible." At that, she wrapped up her bread and cheese and put it back into her pack.

About two weeks later, we were together again sitting at a table with other pilgrims who stopped to rest. As we shared some funny stories that recently occurred, Aileen told us about her experience the day before. She took off a day from walking and was sitting at a small table in a village. Her feet were miserable and the rest of her body not doing very well, either. She ordered a hot chocolate to drink, thinking it might comfort her. As she drank it, Aileen felt something in her mouth. She reached in and pulled it out. To her surprise, she discovered it was a cockroach. Aileen said, "You know what I did? I threw the bug away and drank the rest of my hot chocolate. Can you imagine me doing that? That's how much I cared!" She had come a long way from swatting flies on her lunch to drinking cockroach hot chocolate but that's what the Camino does. It tears the stuffing out of our neat and tidy ways of doing life.

I WISH I COULD SAY that letting go eventually became my natural response. Sometimes I did respond with little difficulty but other times I fell back into my old patterns of clinging and clutching. So much depended on my physical and emotional condition. What did change for me is that I became more aware of how much better the days went when I chucked my wants and expectations and accepted the situation for what it was.

I learned again that no matter how tightly I grasp something I cannot keep it as it is or make it last forever. Holding on with a ferocious grip does not change a situation to match my wants and desires. This tremendous teaching about letting go became clearer to me on the Camino. It taught me not to grasp what's dear to me but to gratefully hold all I value with open hands. Life goes much better that way.

6

REMEMBER:
LIFE IS A GREAT ADVENTURE

Security is mostly a superstition. It does not exist in nature,
nor do the children of humankind as a whole experience it.
Avoiding danger is no safer in the long run than outright
exposure. Life is either a daring adventure, or it is nothing at all.

—Helen Keller

T hat first step on the Camino is one the pilgrim never forgets. It's a thrilling moment that one anticipates with hope and enthusiasm, and with considerable thought about the expectant rigors. Tom told me at the end of our journey that stepping onto the path was the most emotional part of the Camino for him. It was a momentous occasion for me, as well. I remember the two of us walking down the road from El Posada Inn that first morning, trying to find the Camino's route. We weren't sure just where it was located and we hunted a bit in the mist before we saw the sign.

We walked over to the marker and stood there by the path which led into the woods. Tom and I looked at the wooden post beside it which displayed both Camino emblems: the yellow arrow and the scallop shell.[7] Both of us went over and touched the designs of the symbols with joy and a bit of awe, knowing they had guided thousands of pilgrims before us as they stepped onto that significant path.

We spoke enthusiastically about starting out, noting how remarkable it was that we were finally there, ready to begin our great journey. It didn't seem possible that the day we longed for had actually come. Our eyes sparkled with joy and our voices were eager with anticipation. We were *really* going to walk the path that had insistently beckoned to us as we prepared our bodies and spirits for what we were about to do.

That morning as we stood breathing in the vibrant energy of an exciting beginning neither of us was truly aware of the valuable lessons awaiting us as pilgrims. When we stepped onto the Camino we did not hear the silent message announcing how the road not only takes us forward through many physical hills and valleys, but also takes us up the hills and valleys of our minds and hearts, dislodging and rearranging much of what we value and hold dear. We did not understand on that day how the journey would commit us to a venture of both pleasure and pain, of inner reckoning and clearing, of heightened awareness and deepened contemplation, and humbled recognition of our human fragility.

Who knew what the adventure would bring us? We only knew that both of us longed to set out, to discover what it held in store. The journey contained something enticing and we were letting it draw us forward. As we continued to stand there, taking in the reality of being in that place and entering the historical route, the moment was breathtaking and celebratory.

Then, we did it. We started out. My heart pounded as we took those first steps into the woods. Immediately, the welcoming odor of pine trees and the hospitable stillness of the forest greeted us. The energy of the Camino wrapped its arms around us and urged us onward. It was a momentous signal to go forth in trust, to have confidence that the treasures of the road were available to us. We smiled easily and felt euphoric. Even though the backpacks weighed heavily on our backs and our legs soon felt tired as we headed down the mountain, it was still hard to believe we were embarking on this amazing pilgrimage. During the first days of the walk, Tom and I often turned to one another with surprise and joy, enthusiastically saying to the other: "We're on the Camino!"

ONCE I MADE THE DECISION to walk the Camino, I looked forward to the unknown, the challenge, and the spirit of discovery: What would each day bring? How difficult were the Camino's trails? Would my body be able to walk all those miles without harm? How would Tom and I get along with each other during those many weeks? What kind of scenery might there be? What local people and pilgrims would we meet? How would I manage constantly being with other people? What would the villages and cities be like? Would we have time to see the historical sites? Where would we stay? How would we take care of ourselves? Would we stay healthy and avoid falling and hurting ourselves?

Webster's dictionary gives various definitions for *adventure*. Among these are two that best describe the Camino for me: "a bold undertaking in which hazards are to be encountered and the issue is staked upon unforeseen events" and "a remarkable occurrence in one's personal history, a stirring experience . . . "

I wanted to approach the pilgrimage as an adventure more than as an accomplishment. During the first week I wrote in my journal:

> *I think the Camino will be a time to stretch, stretch, stretch. I believe this is just what I needed for my sixtieth year, to take me out of my comfort zone, to teach me about the value of trekking into the unknown, to step out into the indefinite and the unexpected.*

Because the spirit of adventure took over me, it never occurred to me to ask questions of another nature such as: Will I be bored? Will the road lose its enticement? Will I be sorry I did this? Will the journey gradually become humdrum and dreary? Those words and thoughts did not fit into my vocabulary of adventure. I assumed whatever happened would be an opportunity for greater expansion of my life. There was never any question about each day being anything other than an unmitigated gift, a daily occasion holding countless possibilities of growth and newness.

How many adventures we had! Often we turned a bend in a road and wondered what was ahead. We continually paused in amazement at the beauty of scenes before us and relished the variety of people we met. Daily we walked into villages, towns, and cities new to us. We marveled at our bodies' ability to endure the toughness our grueling days required of them. I have written in other chapters of these difficulties, fears, and struggles of the journey. All were part of the adventure.

There were other *unforeseen events* that also gave the journey the flavor of adventure and added to our *stirring experiences* on the Camino. Each place and situation offered us something new: eating foods not common to us such as sopa de verdura, paella, and pulpo, finally getting a book in English to read the last week of the walk *(The Story of Pi),* seeing the city of Santiago loom large before us as we came to our journey's end, meeting pilgrims we thought we'd never see again, and cherishing fresh friendships.

Our adventures were, indeed, many. The body itself had never before known the rigors and challenges it faced as the back embraced the cumbersomeness of the pack and the legs trudged onward, willing themselves to continue in spite of a lack of energy. We walked mile after mile over rough stones, on hot cement and dusty roads, under blazing sun, in the coolness of drizzle and the mugginess of heavy rain. We never listened to a radio and rarely read a newspaper so we had no idea from day to day if it would be hot or cold, dry or wet. Part of the Camino's adventure was to step into the day and receive whatever weather was given to us.

WERE THERE DAYS when I wanted to quit? Yes. Were there times when I thought I was a bit loony for what I was putting myself through? Yes, no doubt about it. But over all, the days were filled, time and again, with the unexpected breath of newness and the recognition that our bodily, mental, and emotional resiliency was capable of meeting the obstacles along the way.

Part of the adventure was the challenge it provided: Would we get beds for the night? What kind of place would we find? Often the challenges were unforeseen until they happened. I recall the first night we stayed in a refugio where the two toilets and two showers were co-ed. I wondered how I would adapt to that and how the other pilgrims would respond to the situation. "Well," I said to myself, "at least there are doors on these showers" and proceeded to hang around the room waiting to see just what to do. I wasn't too comfortable with the thought of coming out of a shower with just a towel around me with all those male strangers nearby. It took some observing of the unspoken rules about who used what room and when but soon I noticed everyone managed just fine. Actually, to my relief, no one seemed to care much as long as we all were clean and found a toilet to use when we needed one.

The Camino also provided a freshness to each day. Every morning as we departed a refugio and reentered the route to Santiago we walked into landscape we had never seen before. If we wanted adventure all we had to do was be intentionally alert and attentive to what was being revealed. The route naturally unveiled daily surprises. We didn't know whom we would meet, what the terrain would be like for walking, or how our bodies would respond. We did not have to seek adventure. It was right there in front of us, beside us, around us. In spite of this, however, we still had to be deliberate about choosing opportunities to enter into the venture.

We almost missed the marvelous trek through Pamplona, which is directly on the Camino's route to Santiago. This was our first big city on the Camino. The night before we were to walk through it, we tossed around the question of whether to take a bus from the edge of the large metropolis or to walk. We thought Pamplona would be congested and it might be difficult to find the arrows or shells to guide us. We still weren't sure what to do as we started out in the morning, but as we walked down the mountain in a soft rain our zest for life revived. We let the spirit of adventure reenter us and decided to keep on walking.

How glad we were that we did not take a bus. The road to Santiago wove through the city and led us into energizing beauty. It was a surprisingly magnificent experience to walk amid

Pamplona's loveliness, past the original ancient city walls being restored, along the government buildings where the running of the bulls is held every year, and through the many green parks with their lovely, colorful flower beds all abloom. It was Sunday and the city was filled with people of various ages and sizes, all enjoying leisurely strolls and outdoor activities.

Three days later, we again made a deliberate choice for adventure by taking a brief detour to the ruins of a castle. In the distance we spied the castle on a high hill when we approached Villamayor de Monjardín. As we got closer and closer to the town, Tom said, "I want to climb up there. Think of the great view we'd have, 360 degrees!" I looked at him like he was crazy. It had to be a good two- to three-mile round trip hike up there. Did he really want us to walk extra miles when we didn't need to? Didn't we get more than enough walking every day? But Tom's adventurous spirit won out. His enthusiasm about the castle whetted my own desire to discover its secrets.

So up we hiked to see what the world looked like from *way up there.* When we arrived, I was immediately glad we had done the extra walking. The top of the hill was like a small park. There were several trees for shade and the area provided a pristine stillness. Much of the old castle ruins remained intact. The tower bell was undamaged, most windows unbroken, one full stone wall was still upright, and several rooms were standing sturdily. The energy around the area was serene. Butterflies flitted among purple star-like flowers and several birds twittered. After we viewed the ruins, we each found our own spot of solitude where we relaxed in sublime quietness. I sat down under an old oak tree, leaned back against it, grateful for the shade and coolness which blessed me on the hot day. Sitting there, I sensed the silent presence of some very old spirits residing among the ruins.

As we walked back down to the village an hour or so later, I was grateful that Tom had encouraged me to join him in the jaunt to the castle. Until we were actually in that lovely space, I did not realize how much I needed its serenity and solitude to regenerate my spirit. I learned that day what a gift it is to have others who will nudge us toward adventure when we aren't willing to enter it ourselves.

There was also a time when we both declined an opportune moment of adventure. On September 21st we walked from Boadilla to Villalcázar de Sirga, where much of the path is lined with willows and poplars along the Ucieza River. It was a humid, windy day. The tall grasses and weeds along the river path added to the stifling air. As we made our way along, we heard voices echoing in the distance.

We came to a clearing on the side of the path where the narrow river was in full view and discovered the voices were coming from women having fun in the river. There, lying naked on their backs in the shallow, refreshing, crystal clear water, were two young German women whom we had met on the road earlier in the day. These two cheerful mermaids waved to us and one of them called, "Why don't you come and join us? It's great in here." We regretfully declined and continued on our way in the steaming afternoon heat. Tom joked the next day, "Not joining those two in the river was our first mistake on the Camino." I laughed and replied, "I think you're right!"

Adventure abounded, however, and there were many opportunities for us to enter into both the joys and the challenges of it. While we wearied of the adversities, we never tired of the surprises the Camino held. When we walked the flat plains of the mesa one day, both of us were extremely fatigued and eager to get to our destination for the day, but we could see nothing that looked like a village on the horizon.[8] We wondered if we read the guidebook inaccurately or miscalculated the miles. Just about the time we thought we'd collapse from exhaustion, hills rose up from the totally flat landscape and there, snuggled in the crevice was the tiny village of Hontanas. What a relief and joy it was to come upon that place of refuge.

THE LOCAL CHURCHES and the Catholic Masses we attended were also quite an adventure. We never knew for sure what we were getting into when we chose to go to Mass. One Sunday we walked into a little village just as the bells of the church rang. From all over the pueblo people came dressed in their good clothes to attend the 11:00 a.m. Mass. We quickly zipped on the pant legs to our shorts (so as not to offend the people with our wearing shorts) and went into the church with the local people. We smiled as the opening song was to the melody of "If I Had a Hammer."

At the end of Mass, I felt lifted back into medieval times. They had a procession with the monstrance in which the consecrated host was placed. The priest held it underneath a canopy extended outward by four men walking alongside it. Another man with a huge, tall, yellow flag and a few other people with lit candles followed. They went to the back of the church and up to the front again while the congregation sang two hymns. Then the host was taken out of the monstrance, put away, and the Mass ended.

Generally, one always knew that a Mass was about to begin by the ringing of church bells. At El Acebo in the late afternoon I was resting in a courtyard when I heard something that sounded like cowbells off key. Ten minutes later, they rang again, just as tinny as before. I thought "it must be a call for Mass." I hurried inside, located Tom in the refugio, and we went down the street to the tiny church.

There were only about a dozen local people, one man and the rest all middle-aged to older women dressed in the dark colors of the pueblos. We sat in a wobbly, wooden pew with an older woman who had some kind of severe illness. Soon after the Mass began, she started to tremble and gradually she shook violently. By the homily time, she had her arms hugged around herself to keep from falling off the pew. I felt so badly for her. She was trembling so much that Tom and I began to shake with her from the movement she created in the rickety pew. Tom whispered, "I think I'm going to get motion sickness." All the people in the little church kept turning around, looking at the shaking woman. Some of them signaled in a compassionate way for her to leave, which she finally did right after the homily. That Mass was an unusual situation, to say the least.

One other church adventure had to do with a local wedding. We arrived in Villalcázar de Sirga in time to see a unique local custom after a wedding Mass. Eight of us pilgrims hung out the upstairs windows in the dormitory and watched the scene. A wedding cake at least four feet tall rested on a platform carried down the street by four men all in white. They were accompanied by musical instruments and much fanfare. I loved watching that scene and being part of the happiness of the local people.

GRADUALLY THE CAMINO helped me see that every day is an adventure because every day is new. We have not lived that day before. Every space of our lives is unknown until we live it. Approaching life in this way keeps it fresh, invigorating, alive, and inviting. There's something marvelous about stepping out each morning and touching new ground every step of the day. Each moment becomes an opening for revelation. Every footstep announces another opportunity for expansion of one's limited version and view of the world. How life-transforming it would be if each of us awakened to the new day with a sense of adventure in our hearts instead of a dread of work or a sluggish approach to what the day holds.

Walking across Spain shook loose the foot-dragging deadness I had in my heart from being too absorbed and obsessed with the crazy busyness of life. It gave me a renewed sense of adventure and enhanced my delight in the ordinary. It allowed for new energy to circulate through the same-stuff-every-day corridors of my life. I learned that adventure is not so much about what we do in our life but how we approach it.

If relationships are stale or work is boring, if life seems dull and lifeless, it is time to brush off old attitudes and worn-out approaches with a sense of adventure. It is time to step outside the borders that have been unconsciously drawn and wake up to what is and can be. Each day is an invitation to look closely, to peer further into the inner regions of what may look like very ordinary moments. Hidden within that ordinariness are the secret jewels of self-knowledge and communion with the Creator.

Adventure depends on openness and an attitude of risk taking. Life can be boring and yawningly predictable or it can be surprisingly eventful and growth-filled. It depends on how we see it and what we allow it to be for us. The landscape of our daily routines may be the same but we are never the same inside. There is always something new waiting for us, if we will only open ourselves to it. What we consider to be everyday and ordinary can have freshness to it if we are willing to enter into it fully. Every day is an adventure daring us to be more fully alive.

7

LIVE IN THE NOW

If I am slavishly attached
to the previous moment
or if I'm already living tomorrow's moments,
then I am not free
for the moment of the eternal now.

—*Macrina Wiederkehr*

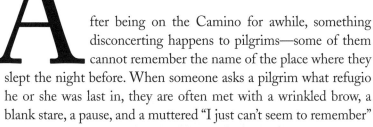

After being on the Camino for awhile, something disconcerting happens to pilgrims—some of them cannot remember the name of the place where they slept the night before. When someone asks a pilgrim what refugio he or she was last in, they are often met with a wrinkled brow, a blank stare, a pause, and a muttered "I just can't seem to remember" or a "Let's see, it was . . . no, that was a couple nights ago. Maybe it was . . . " From a pilgrim's point of view, it is rather consternating the first time this happens. I remember thinking to myself: "Good grief. Am I losing it? All I'm doing here is walking from one place to another. Why can't I remember the name of that last town?"

One simple reason for the inability to remember was that we stayed every night at a different place, one whose name we rarely had heard before we entered the Camino. This was not the central factor, however. Only gradually did I glimpse the deeper reason for the memory lapse. Slowly I came to see that my mind was moving away from the past and steadily focusing on the Now. The first week I wrote in my journal:

> *I do not yet know what this journey is about. Little flashes of insight, teachings, come to me. But all I can do each day is use my energy to walk, to find food and housing. There is very little energy left over. It forces me to live Now.*

After being on the Camino for a week and a half, I experienced more insight into this phenomenon:

My mind seems to be sleepy these days. Met a man from Ireland
and I could not even remember the names of Belfast and Dublin!
Whatever is going on? I rarely think of "home" except when I
name all my loved ones in our morning prayer. Wonder why my
mind resists remembering. I feel as though I really am "on the
Camino" and living in the NOW. My mind doesn't want to go
to the past.

The Camino forces the pilgrim into the present moment.
There's really nowhere else to go. The longer one is on the
Camino, the greater the possibility of developing oneness with the
road and with life. If a pilgrim walks long enough, he or she gradually just walks, just travels, just lives, from one footstep to the
next, entering every moment with greater and greater awareness.
All of one's energies are drawn into the present situation in order
to stay healthy and to walk with a minimum amount of discomfort.

Reading *The Power of Now* by philosopher Eckhart Tolle prepared me for how the Camino draws one to live in the Now. Tolle
teaches that true inner liberation only happens when we let go of
the past and the future and choose to focus on the present.
According to Tolle, in order to enter into personal transformation,
we must be keenly aware of what is going on internally. To do this,
we have to pay more attention to the Now. When our mind is in
the past or the future, we are not aware of what is happening
inside of us at the present moment. By living in the Now we can
discover what stirs within us.

Tom and I both believed in the worth of Tolle's philosophy
and wanted to put it into practice on the pilgrimage. Even so, we
knew it would be much easier to read about it than to live it.
Trying to exist in the Now is a terrific endeavor but it definitely
takes a lifetime of practice and observation. The Camino is a great
place to practice it. The steady rhythm of walking, the focus on
the body's condition, the need to be alert to where one walks, the
long hours of reflection, all allow for living in the Now.

I became convinced of this the day Tom and I walked by a golf course and an urbanization project near Cirneña, which is about three miles outside of Santo Domingo. As we walked past it, Tom commented: "What's a golf course doing out here in the boondocks?" It did seem strange until I thought for a bit and realized we were not in the boondocks. I turned to Tom and informed him, "We're only a five minute drive from the city." He looked a bit stunned, smiled, and said, "You're right. I've become accustomed to *walking time*"—which was another way of saying he was getting more attuned to living in the Now.

WHEN WE WALKED the Camino, my thoughts seldom went backward to home or to the work I left behind. My thoughts went more toward the future: the goal of getting to Santiago, the next refugio, what people we might meet, where we would eat. In continually looking ahead, of course, I was missing what was right before me. When I focused on what was ahead, my mind took over, making positive plans and predicting problems that might never happen. Tolle acknowledges this very thing in his book, *Stillness Speaks:*

> *Almost everyone lives like this most of the time. Since the future never arrives, except as the present, it is a dysfunctional way to live. It generates a constant undercurrent of unease, tension, and discontent. It does not honor life, which is Now and never not Now.*

It took about a week on the Camino before I felt ready to begin to enter into the Now. Slowly the days blended into one another. I could sense something inside of me springing loose. I liked the way it felt. I was feeling freer and more at peace, learning to be content with where the journey led rather than trying to predict and program it to my desires. The longer we walked, the more attentive I was to the present moment. Of course, I readily fell out of the Now but at least I was more aware when this happened.

Most every day I had to deliberately pull my mind away from the future and reorient it to the present. My journal reminded me of this:

It has been a hard day of walking. I did not expect to be so tired each day. I can't have expectations of it. I just need to live NOW. Even this refugio at Estella. At first, when I saw the situation, I said to myself, "Just grit your teeth and think of tomorrow." But then, I said, "No, I must enter into THIS experience, NOW." After I did this, the situation didn't look quite so deplorable and I found I could tolerate it better.

Several things about the Camino continually helped to keep my focus on Now. Packing my backpack every morning was one of them. I paid attention to which things went where. I also had to be sure not to leave anything behind. It was easy to leave laundry on a line outside or a towel hanging on the bedpost, or forget to look under the bed for items that might have slipped there overnight.

The biggest help in being attentive to the Now were the yellow arrows and the scallop shells that constantly pointed to the Camino's route. These arrows guide travelers through all sorts of terrain: mountains, meadows, farm fields, rocky hillsides, little villages, and huge, sprawling cities. They direct pilgrims past garbage dumps, factories, dairies, churches, marketplaces, and most every type of terrain and structure. I read somewhere that the Camino is so well marked it's almost impossible to lose the way. That's basically true but it is quite possible to miss the markers if one is not paying attention.

The arrows and shells give pilgrims' eyes a workout because they are rarely in the same place. These markers are painted on trees, stones, and fence posts, on the tops, bottoms, sides, and corners of buildings. They're etched on sidewalk tiles and scrawled below stop signs. The signs are even on woodpiles and abandoned machinery. Actually, the directional markers are found just about anyplace there's room for paint. The pilgrim has to be awake and watchful for options on the route—such as crossings, intersections, side streets, little roads, or anything that looks like a footpath. One has to be constantly alert, in the NOW moment, wakeful at every option where there's a choice of direction. He or she has to be sure to look and see if there's a marker to indicate straight ahead or to make a turn. Alertness and attentiveness are vital.

There were several times when we missed the signs. Sometimes we were busy talking or unfocused in our quietness and forgot to look, and once in awhile the directional markers confused us. When we left the Puente la Reina refugio we were barely down the street before we were hesitating about the yellow arrows. Strong yellow arrows on the right pointed to a busy highway but there was also a smaller yellow arrow on a tree to our left. It had a black garbage bag around it partially ripped away so the arrow could be seen. Obviously the sign had been covered to indicate the route in that direction was closed. So did the ripped garbage bag mean it was now open? We wondered which way to go.

On a closer look, the sign by the highway had another symbol of a bicycle on it, indicating the road was for Camino bicyclists. So we walkers followed the small arrow to the left. A big mistake. We should have walked to the right, along the highway. A hard rain fell the night before and after half a mile we got into sticky, red, clay mud. What a mess. If it had not been so terribly difficult to maneuver, it might have been quite funny. There we were with about thirty other pilgrims, slipping and sliding up a steep hill. It took tremendous effort to go up and not fall down in the muck. Our whole focus concentrated on trying to maintain our balance. The bottoms of our boots grew thick with the junk, adding more weight to our feet. We continued to go in and out of this mire for over half the day before we came to the blessed relief of a gravel and stone path. In spite of its gooiness, the mess of the mud pulled us into the present moment, forcing us to attend to each step lest we fall into it.

We made our biggest mistake in missing the arrows on the day we walked to Portomarín. We noticed how large and unusually apparent the yellow arrows were that marked our way. Tom said, "These are the biggest and best arrows we've seen on the entire Camino. Let's take a photo of one to show the folks back home so we can explain how much the arrows helped to keep us from getting lost." Everything continued to go well but it was a long day's walk and eventually our bodies and spirits drooped. As we trudged along, we both became quiet. Every once in awhile one of us would groan, "How much further?" or "I didn't think the city was that far away." The more we focused on getting to Portomarín, the less we focused on the Now.

In our anxiety to arrive at where we were going, we grew careless. Eventually, I noticed the city in the distance was on our right when it should have been straight ahead. I started looking closely for arrows and saw none. I turned to Tom in concern and said, "I think we missed an arrow." Tom questioned my suggestion because the markers had been so big and clear all day. We went on walking. Fifteen minutes later, he agreed we must be off track. He volunteered to walk through a small woods to our right and look for a trail toward the city but came back without finding one. We didn't know whether to turn back or to continue ahead. We decided to walk on because it looked like the road would eventually curve and bring us into the city. About then a car came by and the driver assured us we would, indeed, get to Portomarín if we walked another mile or so.

Tom kept trying to figure out just where we had missed the arrow. He went over this the rest of the way into Portomarín. I didn't care how we missed the arrow. I was thinking about the future, talking about my need to get to the refugio and have a rest. Because we both left the present moment and focused on the past and the future, our inner peace and harmony departed.

That is not the end of the lesson, though. Once we got to the refugio we met another pilgrim whose journey meshed with ours several times in other places. She had a way of speaking in soft, abrupt sentences which gave a certain tone of aloofness. We chatted about the day. Then Tom, who was still irritated about missing the arrow, went back to talking about where and how and why we missed it, saying, "I just wish I could figure out where we went wrong." She, in turn, said bluntly: "It doesn't make any difference. You are where you're supposed to be."

Bop! Her comment was like a whack on the side of the head. I don't know if she realized it but she moved Tom and me back into the Now. Because she directed her frank remark to Tom, he was especially annoyed with it. At dinner that evening, we talked about what she said to us. I felt her words held a teaching but Tom was not so sure. By the next day, however, her message took hold. As we walked away from Portomarín, Tom mused, "I always need to know why and where I went wrong. That's not necessary. It's enough to know we were not attentive, that we need to be more aware, and then move on. I have to let go of knowing where that arrow was."

The Portomarín incident was more than a Camino event. It taught me that when any of us is not focused and attentive to the Now, we lose our way. We miss the direction for our life's journey. We can easily get lost in the past or in the future when things don't go the way we hope or plan for them to go. The arrows and scallop shells are symbols of the habits and disciplines we need to develop in our daily lives to keep us constantly turning toward the Now. Hanging onto things of the past or anxiously anticipating the future only leads to less peacefulness. The energy of life's road springs forth in what happens on the way. This is where our life lessons lie, not in what we leave behind nor in what we have yet to attain.

As the days of the Camino went on, we kept reminding one another about needing to live in the Now. If we noticed one of us getting off track, we gently brought the other one back. Each of us also had our own personal way of practicing this exercise. I was constantly drawn back to the present by being deliberately attentive to nature and to life around me. Tom's practice was to give himself little messages. He told me he was trying to develop the habit of saying "I am not in the future—I am in the Now" whenever he found himself feeling distressed or anxious. He also confided that each day he was seeking to "go deep into the presence of God's being and rest there, to let God heal my aches and soothe my body and my spirit."

Tom's comments were a great help for moving me to a deeper place. I saw how living in the Now leads me into a stronger union with God because it is a way of constant openness to divine grace. When I am attentive to the Now, I am able to be more open and receptive interiorly. God is with me in the present moment. It is *here* that this Goodness reaches into my life and beckons to me. The Now provides what I need to respond to God and to life wholeheartedly.

8

BE ATTENTIVE TO YOUR BODY

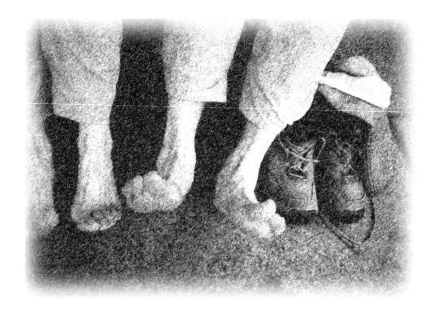

Blessed be our feet that feel the beat
at the heart of life.

—*Joy Mead*

Blisters! Big ones! I read numerous descriptions in the Camino literature about the gruesome possibility of these unwanted creatures. One author told of seeing silver-dollar-sized ones on a pilgrim's foot. If this wasn't enough to convince me to avoid them on my own feet, I was convinced when I actually saw these blisters on other pilgrims' feet. I winced when I saw a young American caressing his foot after a long day. He moaned as he stuck a needle through the huge, pus-filled blister covering his entire heel.

To ensure that our feet would be blister free, Tom and I searched out good hiking boots. In December I found a pair on sale. They were a bit uncomfortable but most boots are until they're broken in. I presumed this was the case for mine. I walked every day in those hiking boots for three months. Finally I admitted they were killing my feet. Calluses developed. Corns on my little toes hardened. Anticipation turned to anxiety. I decided if I kept using those boots my feet would be ruined before I ever walked the Camino.

Tom was also having problems with his boots. He told me about some new ones at Beaverdale Back Country, a store where we bought most of our equipment. The day I went to check on those boots was a joyful day for my feet. I found a pair of Garmonts, a new style with a wide front area that was much more humane. My toes loved those boots.

It was not just boots, however, that kept my feet blister free on the Camino. My friend Bill sent me an article about a couple in Arizona who recently returned from the pilgrimage. I couldn't believe what I read. One of them used Vaseline on her feet. She stopped every two or three miles, took off her boots and socks, and greased up. She insisted she never got a blister. I bought some Vaseline. I'd try anything.

THEN I HEARD SOMETHING even stranger. A young woman in Des Moines who walked the Camino a year or so before us said she used duct tape. Well, I knew duct tape was good for just about everything, but blister prevention? Sue told us that whenever she felt a "hot spot" on her foot, which was an indication of a blister preparing to form, she stopped to put a piece of duct tape on that spot to prevent further abrasion.

Amazingly, not one blister developed on our feet in our 450 miles. Much of this good fortune was due to the sound advice we received from those two women. Tom and I stopped every three or four miles, took our boots and socks off, aired our feet, and applied either Vaseline or duct tape. I must admit that when I looked at my greasy feet with the little pieces of red duct tape on them, I smiled at how ridiculous they looked. But it worked! As I took time tending to my feet before I put my boots on each morning, I often thought: "If I am good to my feet, my feet will be good to me." And they were.

Besides blisters, I was concerned about possible dehydration. Keeping sufficient moisture in the body not only lessened the possibility of blisters forming, it also guaranteed stamina and energy. One pilgrim I met collapsed on the Camino because of a lack of water so I was a bit compulsive about having a sufficient supply of it. I carried three bottles at all times, each holding twenty-four ounces. The bottles added a lot of weight to my pack but I didn't care. Water was precious to me. Most days I would not have had to carry so much. Almost every village had an open fountain where we could refill our bottles. There were occasional days, however, when we walked for over half a day without ever catching sight of a fountain.

ON THE HOT, DRY MESA dehydration was a particular issue for our bodies because there was so little shade. The possibility of sunstroke or collapsing from lack of moisture was real. I was thirsty most of the time. Another pilgrim counseled us about having enough potassium in our systems when Tom and I both complained of being exceptionally tired. She suggested that the strenuous days coupled with the high heat might be depleting our systems of this important mineral. With bananas often unavailable, we bought some potassium pills the next day. They then became a regular part of our daily diet. I don't know if they made a significant difference but we both felt better.

During those weeks on the mesa, we protected our bodies as much as possible from the powerful rays of the sun. Tom and I heeded the guidebook's advice about wearing hats on the Camino not only to protect our facial skin, but to keep us cooler. I chose a wide-brimmed hat to give me lots of protection. Tom's was much smaller but it seemed to provide what he needed. It was so hot on those days that he sometimes took his hat off and poured some precious water into it to keep his head cooler. We also slathered sunscreen on us to avoid a nasty burn.

On the mesa and everywhere else on the Camino, stopping to rest was vital. It was a continual challenge to not keep pushing on and ignore how our bodies felt. Walking in a relaxed manner was crucial. Stopping to rest slowed us down, which meant it took longer for us to reach our day's destination. However, it also assured us we would walk with more energy, as well as promising our legs and feet less soreness and fatigue.

Resting is not an American trait. Siesta is not in our lifestyle. If anything, needing to rest is seen as a weakness. ("Oh, you need a nap? Too bad. Something must be wrong with you.") Tom and I learned that taking a quiet pause of ten or twenty minutes refreshed our bodies and also refreshed our spirits. Because of this, we walked the extensive miles each day with greater ease and with less of a spirit of grudging endurance.

Another huge "body lesson" pertained to sleep deprivation. Walking twelve to eighteen miles day after day was exhausting. At the end of the day my legs ached, my feet were hot and sore, and my back and shoulders were greatly fatigued from carrying my backpack. When I got into the bunk bed at night, I simply collapsed and "died to the world." I almost always had at least eight hours of sleep on the Camino, which was quite different from my six and a half at home. Snoring, harsh overhead lights, and numerous noises rarely kept me awake once my head hit the pillow. When I awoke in the morning, I was astounded at how much better I felt. Though it might still be stiff and sore, my body was ready to walk again. The exhaustion of the previous night was gone. Sleep continually gifted me with renewed resiliency and strength.

Our backpacks also taught us lessons about caring for our bodies. Boots and backpacks were our key equipment priorities and we chose both well. Still, Tom and I had days when our packs caused us discomfort. Tom spent almost a week working to figure out where the pressure point on the pack was that caused him dreadful discomfort and backaches. Between the two of us we finally got his pack adjusted adequately.

A week or so after that, my pack gave me constant problems. For three days my shoulders and back were filled with pain. I tossed and moved the pack on my back as I walked along. I pulled the straps tighter, then looser, stopped to move the weight around inside, worked with the hip belt, put my hands under my pack to hold the weight out away from me, kept lifting the straps off my shoulders, and tugged at every adjustable part of it. I tried everything. On and on my struggle went. I just couldn't get my pack to feel comfortable.

Shoulder and back irritability seeped into my spirit. There, too, I felt ill-tempered, grouchy, and upset. On the third day of these troubles I awoke and definitely did not want to put that backpack on again. As I was dressing, I remembered the wisdom of *befriending and learning from whatever it is that irritates us.* I decided to name the backpack "Sophicitta," a combination of Greek and Spanish meaning "little wisdom." That is the day my backpack irritability basically ended. I readjusted the straps and the items inside one more time and it worked.

Even though there were plenty of future days when my pack felt overly heavy, I never had the imbalance and constant thrashing about that I had in previous days. In naming the backpack I turned toward it rather than against it. In befriending my backpack, it was no longer an enemy of mine. In doing so, I was able to use personal energy more positively and patiently, becoming clear-headed in seeing what needed to be changed. On the morning of naming my pack I discovered I was consistently putting my tennis shoes in the wrong spot. I decided to move one to each side instead of placing them on top of each other. This adjustment created a much better balance. It was the *way* I arranged my pack, not the pack itself, that caused my body discomfort.

There were other body lessons to be learned. One of the things Tom and I had a good laugh over was that for all our care and attention to our bodies, we missed what they were telling us completely about mid-way into the journey. One day we stopped to take a breather. Tom pointed to his legs and exclaimed: "Look! I don't have bandy-rooster legs anymore. All this walking has finally given me muscle." We both laughed as he went on and on about this physical change.

I then took a look at my legs and gasped at what I saw. Mine, too, had firmed and developed a lot of muscle. Only mine looked like large, round fence posts. I moaned and groaned about this development and we laughed some more. We promptly forgot about our muscled legs as we continued onward. It was several weeks later before we realized that what we took for "muscle" was actually swelling from all the walking we had done on the hot mesa. By the time we reached Santiago, Tom reclaimed his bandy-rooster legs and I happily ended the fence-post stage.

This inability to accurately recognize what was happening to our bodies ought not to have surprised us. Paying attention to our bodies and tending to their needs was not something that either of us grew up with in our homes. The unspoken motto of my own family in regard to the body was "Tough it out. If you ignore it long enough, it will heal itself." I don't think my farmer dad ever spent a day in bed from illness even though he had the flu and bad colds like the rest of us. One time when I was a young teenager I was riding on the tractor with him when a huge bumblebee got caught in my sleeve and stung me four times. I yelled and tears filled my eye. My dad looked over at me and said, "Oh, it doesn't hurt *that* much, does it?"

So I grew up basically ignoring what my body felt and needed. It was not until I was well into my adult years that I learned the value and importance of being kind to this important part of myself. By the time I headed to the Camino, I valued eating well and taking the time to exercise but there were still areas where I neglected my physical temple. Sufficient sleep and pausing to rest were low on my list of bodily care and maintenance.

WEEKS OF WALKING the Camino showed me how I failed to give myself sufficient sleep. Since my return from Spain, I deliberately get more sleep. A part of my calm and energy since the Camino is due to this lesson of taking care of the whole "me." I discovered that sleep is a magnificent healer and restorer of energy, a gift never to be taken for granted. On the days when I am rested, I look at the day's problems with a positive attitude. During times when I am tired and drowsy, my enthusiasm quickly wanes and it is much easier for me to whine when things do not go as planned.

Studies show that many Americans are sleep deprived. They still subject the body to their overly full schedules, eat too much fast food, omit exercise due to time pressures, and rarely get adequate amounts of sleep to restore their body's energy balance. The Camino taught me that the body is more than a frame or a house for the soul. The body is an integral part of us. If we boss and push our body around for too long, or subject it to our whims of overwork and lack of leisure, we become more and more off-balance and unhealthy in our mental and emotional capacities as well.

BEING ATTENTIVE to the needs of the body was a very important life lesson on the Camino. When I was on the pilgrimage I tried to treat my body as a "thou," offering my compassion when there was pain and soreness, giving thanks when there was health and energy. Each day I grew in appreciation for my body's helpfulness and resiliency. I gained a new sense of wonder at how the human body does all it can to assist us physically, no matter how lacking or inadequate our care might be.

I thought I knew how much my body's condition affected my mental, emotional, and spiritual well-being but I had to relearn that important truth on the Camino. I became even more convinced that my body and spirit are friends, not enemies. Each influences the other to be alive and alert. How I feel physically affects how I am on other levels of my being. My *self* is a whole *self*, not a *self* with many individual compartments that exist separately. I now know if I am to have peace and well-being, I cannot ignore either body or spirit on my life's journey.

When I returned home from the Camino, most of the skin on the bottom of both my feet sloughed off. That this would happen was not surprising. My soles had been red, swollen, and hot for the last two weeks of walking. I thought the sloughing off was symbolic. While the soles of my feet were letting go of old, dead skin, I was letting go of old, dead ways of treating and tending to myself.

9

ACKNOWLEDGE THE KINDNESS OF STRANGERS

The true essence of humankind is kindness.
There are other qualities which come from
education or knowledge, but it is essential, if one
wishes to be a genuine human being and impart
satisfying meaning to one's existence, to have a good heart.
—*The 14th Dalai Lama*

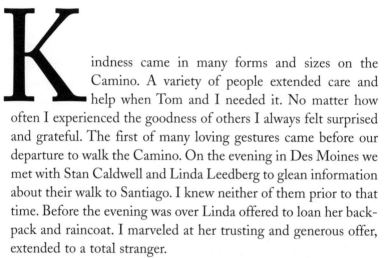

Kindness came in many forms and sizes on the Camino. A variety of people extended care and help when Tom and I needed it. No matter how often I experienced the goodness of others I always felt surprised and grateful. The first of many loving gestures came before our departure to walk the Camino. On the evening in Des Moines we met with Stan Caldwell and Linda Leedberg to glean information about their walk to Santiago. I knew neither of them prior to that time. Before the evening was over Linda offered to loan her backpack and raincoat. I marveled at her trusting and generous offer, extended to a total stranger.

Day after day on the Camino strangers reached out to help. Both pilgrims and local people presented kindnesses to us constantly. A young clerk in Arres actually left her place at the cash register in the supermercado after Tom asked for directions to the Asador restaurant. She happily took Tom by the sleeve, led us out of the store, down to the end of the street, and pointed us in the direction of the restaurant. Then she smiled and waved goodbye as we headed up the street.

Another day, as we walked from Ventosa to Azofra, we noticed a short, elderly man stooped over in a vineyard, attentively working among ripening rows of grapevines. It was about 8:30 a.m. and we had been walking over an hour without breakfast. Just seeing the beautiful grapes made my mouth water. "What do you think he's doing?" Tom asked. "You're asking me?" I replied. "I know nothing about growing grapes, only fields and fields of Iowa corn!" Tom laughed and suggested we go and ask the man himself so we moved off the path and walked into the vineyard, down the row to where he was busily working. The old man smiled widely when he looked up and became aware of us. He greeted us graciously with "Hola" (hello), revealing a mouth with just one tooth in it. The diligently working farmer did not seem to mind our approach interrupting his work.

As we stood beside the wizened man between the rows of grapes he had been cutting and tossing onto the ground, Tom asked, "What are you doing with the grapes? We've been watching as we walked along and we're curious as to why you're cutting some of the clusters off the vines. They look fine to us. Is there something wrong with them?" The little man explained he was pruning out the unripe and damaged grapes before the harvest a week or so away. The little man's face and voice held such warmth and pride as he enlightened us and talked about his vineyard. Then he reached over to one of the beautiful vines and cut off two large bunches of ripened purple grapes. As he held them out for us to take, I thought: "This man owes us nothing. We strangers interrupted his progress and here he is sharing the bounty of his hard work." It wasn't our intent to receive food from this kind man and we thanked him profusely as we walked away with a luscious breakfast in our hands.

The bountiful vineyards are one example of the beautiful and abundant food grown in northern Spain. Because I enjoy vegetables so much, I often looked longingly at them when we walked by magnificent gardens laden with produce. One day shortly before noon Tom and I noticed a good-sized garden of plenty on a flat section by a creek. Just beyond the garden was a high hill where another elderly Spanish man slowly toted two big bags overflowing with fresh vegetables. Because the day was steamy hot and the road steep, the man stopped periodically to rest the heavy bags on the road.

When I saw him with the weighty bags, I felt badly for the tired elder and wanted to help carry the vegetables up the hill. I also thought the situation offered a good opportunity to practice speaking Spanish. As I greeted him, the man turned and grinned. Although he declined my offer of help, he took the opportunity to rest a bit. When he set his bags down, I noticed several yellow and red tomatoes as big as two fists mixed in with the rest of the vegetables. While we each commented about the weather, he dug out a tomato with wide, open ridges on the top and explained, "Too much water." Then the soft-spoken gentleman picked up one of his largest tomatoes and offered it to me. My gut response was to refuse, thinking how heavy the gift would be to carry. The tomato must have weighed a pound. The man's kindness was so real, however, I knew I could not refuse. As I walked away with the huge tomato, the generous stranger beamed with pleasure.

When we were on the bus to León an older woman with a lovely, purple flowered dress and woolen sweater sat across the aisle from me. She kept watching me and smiling. After about ten minutes she motioned to me and showed me how to put the arm rest up by my seat, which made the ride much more comfortable.

The restaurateur at the café near the León bus station was extremely patient with us when Tom and I could not make up our minds as to which sandwich we wanted. After we left the café, we were halfway down the block when the same person ran out, called after me, and brought the walking staff I left behind. "Wow," I remarked to Tom afterward, "he didn't have to do that. What's a pilgrim's staff to him?" That simple gesture of kindness meant a lot to me because my walking stick was essential for climbing hills and going over rough patches of stones. The simple, good deed saved me from possibly twisting an ankle or falling and breaking bones.

At the refugio in Triacastela, we were elated to discover they actually had a washing machine but then we realized we had no soap. The refugio director overheard our conversation and gave us two cubes of soap. Later, he came around to check on the rooms. Tom was resting on his bunk bed when the director came in and saw Tom shivering. It was unusually cold that day and the man returned a short while later with a blanket, placed it on top of Tom and playfully tucked him in. When Tom thanked him with, "Como mi mamá" (like my mother), the man smiled and dismissed his kindness with, "You're a pilgrim."

We found other local people equally helpful. Waitresses and waiters gave us advice on local customs about tipping and not tipping. Shop keepers advised us on where to find daily necessities. Other people helped us locate banks, post offices, churches, and pharmacies. Pedestrians who passed by and people in cars greeted us with "Buen Camino!" which often served to encourage and lift our spirits when fatigue set in.[9] Everywhere we experienced the kindness of the Spanish people.

Tom and I received constant kindness from other pilgrims, too. Often the pilgrims' kindness showed itself not only in the help they gave us but also in their generous gestures of care and concern. One beastly hot day we walked from Tosantos to Atapuerca. Because of the heat, most pilgrims stopped before Atapuerca to stay at San Juan de Ortega. Because it was only midafternoon, Tom and I decided to go on another three and a half miles to the village of Atapuerca before ending the day's journey. As we walked out of the town, a New Zealander named Colette ran after us, urging us not to go further, saying she feared we might collapse from the heat. We assured her that our training in the Iowa humidity and heat conditioned us for just such a walk. In spite of her compassionate pleas, we kept on going.

When we first arrived in Atapuerca, I said to Tom, "We should have listened to Colette's advice" because by the time we arrived the small refugio with twenty-two beds was full. Tom and I were drained from the heat when we walked in and discovered we had no place to stay. Walking on further to another town was impossible in our condition. The pilgrims in the refugio, especially a young, sensitive Swiss named Karl, expressed alarm for us. Karl suggested, "Why don't you try the restaurant? They might have some rooms above it. We'll help you find something. Don't worry." The look of concern on Karl's face told me he would do all he could for us. Tom and I went down the street to the restaurant and found three single beds still available. We no sooner discovered this when Karl appeared at the door to check on us, explaining, "I needed to be sure you two found a place to stay." He seemed as relieved as we were.

Numerous other pilgrims reached out to us. Everyone helped Tom search for and find his billfold when he lost it in the refugio at Villamayor de Monjardín. Nurses from England shared their medical tape for our sore feet when I inadvertently left mine behind. Experienced pilgrims advised which path to take when we faced options and decisions. A pilgrim called out to me with a warning one day as I absentmindedly filled my water bottle from a fountain where a sign noted the water in the fountain was dangerous to drink. A young German pilgrim opened a costly bar of rich chocolate he carried all day and shared the delicious contents with us.

LITTLE KINDNESSES also came our way from overseers in the refugios. A lot of these people were volunteers who experienced the solicitous care of strangers when they walked the Camino. These pilgrims came back with the intention of offering similar hospitality to new pilgrims on the road. Three volunteers at the English refugio at Rabanal del Camino not only took care of registration but showed us to where the bunk beds were located. As they did so, they asked about our pilgrimage, offered to help us with things we might need, gave us directions for where to buy food, and assured us by their care that they valued us and our journey. The spirit of friendliness of these three was balm for our tired bodies and spirits.

Hostelers also volunteered helpful information from their experience of walking the Camino. One day before traveling from

Triacastela to Sarria, we stopped at the other refugio in town to use the internet. We debated about taking an alternate route to see the Monasterio de Samos, an ancient, enormous monastery which the guidebook mentioned. When we asked the volunteer about the site, we learned he was an architect and his advice convinced us the monastery's touted structural design was much overrated. With this information, we made a decision not to take the alternate route and saved ourselves an extra five or six miles of walking.

At Villalcázar de Sirga the woman who directed the refugio went to her own storage space and gave me a toothbrush when I asked where I could purchase one. I forgot mine in the bathroom at the last place and because it was Sunday, she knew the stores were closed. I offered to pay her for the toothbrush but she just smiled and said, "No, a gift for you."

SIMILAR KINDNESSES often occurred when Tom asked refugio directors if there were any lower bunk beds available when we registered for the night. Because Tom got up several times to use the bathroom, top bunks in the dark of night were difficult for his sixty-nine-year-old body to maneuver. One time a director led him to a small room with a cot he could use. Another time a director led Tom to a separate area where there was a room right next to the bathroom. I teased him by saying, "It's your fluent Spanish and baby blue eyes that get you all these special perks," but we both knew it was the thoughtfulness and goodness of the hostelers that blessed him with these small but essential requirements of life.

My strongest memory of a pilgrim's kindness on the Camino has to do with a thin, quiet, middle-aged Spaniard named Carlos who came to my assistance. Carlos's pigeon-toed gait and spindly legs made his walking even slower than our unhurried pace. For several days in a row we passed by him, each time commenting quietly to ourselves on his courage as he tried to walk the entire route, given his weak physique. Carlos rarely engaged in any extended conversation and seemed to enjoy his solitary pilgrimage. Although he spoke little, he was always courteous and full of smiles when we happened to be together at a fountain filling water bottles or when we met in the evenings at the refugios.

When we stayed at Boadilla, Tom and I got up long before dawn to begin walking because it was so hot in that region. In order to not awaken other pilgrims we dressed in the dark. Then we took our boots and packs out to another room where there was a meager bit of light to finish getting ready. Carlos sat at a round, wooden table eating his breakfast, a kind of gruel he prepared every day. I bid him good morning and sat down to put some Vaseline on the tender spots of my feet. Then we left quietly with a whispered "Buen Camino" to him.

Around midmorning we stopped at a village to rest on an old brick wall. We had walked about three hours so it was time for us to take off our boots and air our feet. I wanted to put some Vaseline on my toes. What a shock I received after much searching and burrowing around in my pack. "Tom, I don't have my Vaseline and tape!" He told me to look some more. "No, I've looked through everything. It's not here. How could I be so stupid and leave it behind? What will I do?" The loss especially distressed me because I could not easily find what I needed in the tiny villages ahead. There was nothing to do but go on, however, and make the best, or worst, of it. I dreaded the thought of blisters. Tom tried to reassure me, "Look, I bet someone will find those things and bring them along. They'll show up again. How about praying to St. Anthony?" "Okay," I muttered. "I'll try anything," but I didn't believe my precious little cargo would ever be returned.

Because we wanted a half day of rest, we stopped early in the afternoon to find housing at Villalcázar de Sirga. No sooner were we settled than the refugio's volunteer supervisor came to the room and announced, "There's a phone call for the two

Americans." I felt immediate dread, thinking something happened to a loved one back home. Who knew us and why else would we receive a phone call? By the time we located the phone, the person calling left a message.

The note told us Carlos was carrying my little bag of foot care items. Because he did not stop at Villalcázar de Sirga as we did, Carlos unknowingly passed us and moved on ahead. He left a message that "the American woman's lost things" could be picked up at the Calzadilla de la Cueza refugio the next day. I was absolutely astonished, totally humbled, and deeply grateful for Carlos's efforts on my behalf. "Just think, Tom," I marveled, "Carlos made the effort to find the name of the place and phone number to give us this message."

The next day we passed through Calzadilla de la Cueza but the director insisted nothing had been left there and dismissed me rather curtly. I was disappointed but there was nothing to do except keep walking. About three miles further on I became violently ill and could hardly walk by the time we arrived at Ledigos in the late afternoon. When we came into the refugio I looked for the nearest mattress to collapse on. Before going upstairs, who came to greet me but Carlos, holding out my lost items! I put my arms around him and began to cry, overwhelmed by his kindheartedness in the midst of my misery.

THE KINDNESS OF STRANGERS on the Camino became a constant teacher for me. Each gesture of goodness stood out as a lesson in love. Each opportunity to receive an unexpected gift of care was an occasion to grow in both amazement and awareness of how powerful these simple gestures can be. They not only provide for a need, they also bring hope to the heart.

The Camino made it easy to be totally present to the kindness of others because life was uncomplicated and the days were basically unencumbered. I was much more attuned to the times when help was given to me Back home now in a much busier schedule, I need to make an effort to be alert to daily kindnesses and not just ignore or brush them off when they occur. When I am totally engaged in MY activities, MY work, MY shopping, MY schedule, MY life, how easily I ignore the goodness extended to me by another. I can distractedly dismiss someone's opening the door for me or giving the gift of a smile. I too easily read hurriedly through gracious letters received or half-listen to phone calls bringing me good news or a message of support.

How much each of us misses when we overfocus on life's busyness. Many times the kindness is there. We only need to receive it with awareness. A simple gift of concern may be just what we need on a weary day. It lifts our spirit when we are consumed with activity, gives us hope in our discouragement, reminds us someone loves us when we feel ragged and torn inside, and helps restore our belief in the goodness of others.

The kindness extended to us by strangers takes us into a larger circle of life. We become conscious of those we meet each day as our companions on the pilgrimage of life. Their caring gestures unite us at a deeper level. When a gift of helpfulness is extended to us, it reminds us that the human heart is a reservoir of love. When kindness is received with awareness, we enter into the reality of being one great family of humanity. Each of us is called to give and receive this precious gift that brings light to the darkest places and soothes the greatest sorrows.

10
DON'T LET DIFFICULTIES DETER YOU

I confess we are a little apprehensive.
We know all too well the difficulties of the way,
and seemed to have forgotten
the joys and blessings of the Camino.

—*Austin Repath*

P lenty of disconcerting difficulties popped up on the Camino. Some problems resulted from simple inconvenience. A few derived from unforeseen situations. Most of the difficulties I experienced were like irritating pebbles in a shoe. On occasion, they felt more like boulders but none came close to the Camino's really big difficulties: serious illness, broken bones from falls, heart attacks, being hit by passing vehicles, and other tragic situations that sometimes resulted in death.

As I reviewed my journal, the number of irritating pebbles astonished me. Not that I forgot the troubles the path insists on giving the pilgrim—they were too insistent for me to forget. Rather, I view them differently now in the light of their spiritual teachings. These impediments of the pilgrimage have taken on a more positive hue because I understand the Camino's power to transform the pilgrim. Struggles are the fertilizer for spiritual growth.

Troubles definitely do abound on the Camino. Unwanted and unexpected tribulations simply cannot be avoided as one walks to Santiago anymore than they can be bypassed in day to day living. No amount of control or guarded lifestyle keeps each moment contained, orderly, and unflawed. There are bound to be upsetting and distressful times. Many of these difficulties are unavoidable due to the nature of the journey. If pilgrims are intent on spiritual growth they cannot ignore these unwanted teachers because they arise daily to confront the traveler, always offering another life lesson along the way.

ONE OF THE MAJOR DIFFICULTIES did not surprise me. I had suspected food to be a problem before I ever started to walk the Camino. "Not having healthy food" was on the list of fears I compiled as I prepared for the pilgrimage. Finding food, having enough food, going hungry or starving were not the only issues I feared about food as I walked from place to place. I was equally concerned about the kind of food. Back home, I was attentive to daily nutrition, eating sufficient vegetables and fruits, low-fat food, and almost no red meat. Soon after being on the Camino I realized I needed to change the way I ate.

Most of the food on the menú del dia, the pilgrim meals at bars and restaurants, offered red meat fried in oil, sometimes drenched in oil (veal, beef, and lots of pork). As we walked further westward, fish became one of the options. These meals were filling and substantial and offered to pilgrims at a low price. After weeks of the same three or four choices for each meal, however, everything begins to taste the same to pilgrims unless they choose to eat at more expensive restaurants where the food is outstanding.

During our thirty-seven days Tom and I opted once for a magnificent evening meal at a hotel. Unfortunately, it was when I had a wretched cold and could hardly enjoy the tasteful food. We also stopped once in the middle of the day to have a splendid lunch in Cacabelos. We stuffed ourselves with fabulous food. The first course was a "tortilla" of sliced potato and egg with a marvelous tomato sauce. The next course was corned beef with cabbage, onion, garbanzo beans, and potatoes. The spices were just right. Finally, we had a local specialty for dessert: vanilla ice cream with a rich chestnut sauce. Unfortunately, we still had several hours to the next refugio after that meal. We learned how tough it is to walk with a stomach full of rich food as we dragged ourselves along.

THE REST OF THE TIME on the Camino our meals were simple. I did not find many fresh vegetables that carried lightly or well in my backpack although I did manage to tote carrots and tomatoes.

Nutritious almonds and walnuts provided super energy but quite a few stores did not sell them. I accepted the extra weight of an apple or a nectarine in my pack. Breakfast offered another challenge. A good bowl of cereal or oatmeal was nowhere to be found. Finding toasted bread was a rare treat. The few times toast was served with butter and jam seemed like a mini-miracle. Much of the time breakfast was dry bread or a sweet treat like a packaged apple turnover. Sometimes we ate no breakfast if bars were not open and we had not planned well enough to have food with us.

Unlike food, lack of privacy tended to be more of an inconvenience than a real difficulty. I quickly learned I could approach the privacy issue as a big problem or as a natural part of refugio living. I did not think a lot about what it might be like to dress and undress in the dormitories before I stayed in them. Maybe I didn't want to think about it. There is no privacy anywhere in refugios, no place where one can really be alone because they are packed with pilgrims. Most certainly privacy is not in the bathrooms where three or four pilgrims usually wait at sinks and by the showers. You wash your face, put on your deodorant, floss and brush your teeth, and do all those personal toiletry things right there in front of everyone else.

Nothing about the body is very private when you are a pilgrim. Besides changing clothes in front of everyone and sharing bathrooms, there is illness. There's talk about sore throats and phlegm, vomiting and diarrhea, constipation and bowel movements. When one pilgrim starts coughing and has a cold, you can be pretty sure the rest of the pilgrims sleeping in the same area will end up with a similar virus.

DURING MY FIRST WEEK on the Camino I smiled to myself one night as I remembered my first years after entering the convent. In the early sixties, the rule requiring no communication with other members during silence times was strictly enforced. We were taught to avoid entering into silent communication with another by "keeping custody of the eyes." This meant casting our eyes downward to avert any direct eye contact.

That first week in the refugios I finally understood the worth of this rule. With little space between bunk beds, even if one changed clothes while on (or in) the bunk bed, there was basically no privacy. During my first evenings on the Camino, I noticed there was no gawking around (well, I gawked a little, discreetly, of course, to see what the situation was!). No undue attention was given to anyone else. Whether there were eighty or four in a room, pilgrims adjusted to living in open space while tending to their personal needs. After awhile I no longer concerned myself about the lack of privacy because it was simply part of being a pilgrim.

The toilet situation was another source of difficulty for me. I never managed to fully accept the dirty state of these rooms. Even if a pilgrim found some privacy in a bathroom or toilet area, no one wanted to stay any longer than absolutely necessary. What a shock to find the restrooms dirty, with inches of water on the floor from showers, no soap or hand towels by the sink. In my previous travels to other countries, I recognized how overly hygienic Americans tend to be. I asked myself if my distaste for the dirt was my Americanism at its worst or if those responsible for the refugios needed to improve the hygiene. I finally decided I could be less finicky but overall the dirt was unnecessary and unhealthy.

The grunge in the refugio restrooms raised a question about basic cleanliness. One shower and bath area in O Cebreiro did not have a window or any other ventilation. The sign said to keep the door shut at all times. The second week I met a woman in her thirties who walked all the way from Germany. She confided to me, "I am disgusted with the refugios in Spain. They are much worse than anywhere else." This comment consoled me a bit (misery loves company) but I also felt called to get used to the situation and stop complaining. A small voice inside told me this difficulty, too, was the Camino's way of helping me to grow.

Another irritation pertained to the lack of toilet paper. The restrooms usually held some paper when the refugios first opened. By the time the throng of pilgrims arrived and unpacked, and everyone used the toilets, the supply of paper was gone and rarely replaced. In no time at all, I ascertained the necessity of stuffing my pockets full of toilet paper if I was going to have some for my nightly trips to the restroom. (I was back home several months before I stopped attempting to put extra toilet paper in my pockets when I was in a public restroom!)

The difficulty of dirty bathrooms rarely abated all the way to Santiago. About the time I thought the situation got better, I found another icky one like the one at Arca. When a pilgrim told me where to locate the refugio's private restroom, I thought, "Wow! This is uptown!" However, it turned out to be no different than the others. In fact, it was worse. Small piles of dirt edged the room looking as if it had not been cleaned in weeks. When I ran water in the sink, sewage odor and brown water surged from a floor drain. As I looked at the water nearing my feet, I saw huge hairballs floating on it.

Showers were a challenge of their own. How grateful I was for my flip-flops when I saw the shower areas. Each place had its own shower system. One or two places had unisex shower rooms but at least the stalls there were private ones. Most had hot water but in one refugio we had to put a coin in for warm water. One day I wrote in my journal:

> *Today's was the topper. I went into the shower. Had just gotten ready to turn on the water and the lights went out. Every two minutes, no lights! I had to keep stepping out of the shower in the dark, open the door, reach around and turn the light on. Then, every two minutes the hot water quit. So I had to turn off the faucet, wait, then turn it back on. And the shower itself, the grime, the rusty edges around the bottom, etc. Not pleasant.*

Housing presented its own set of difficulties. Refugios did not accept reservations. As much as Tom and I tried, we often felt a bit of tension about where we would stay until we actually checked in and had our bunk beds or mattresses for the evening. Finding a bed wasn't the only problem about housing. As the days and weeks went by, the night odors in the rooms grew worse. I'd get up at night for a bathroom break and discover stale, dead air in the room. I opened the door or window but someone else invariably closed the window because of a draft or got up and shut the door.

Along with low oxygen levels, the dormitory rooms contained body odors and smells from food in backpacks. (My own pack sometimes reeked from the goat cheese I carried.) In a few instances, we were required to put our boots by the front door but most times pilgrims wore their boots into the dormitory area. Foot and boot odors added to the unpleasant fragrance. On the days we tromped through cow and sheep manure, the rankness in the room grew pungent, indeed.

Besides the housing situation, we walked long distances day after day. The path included walking on large stones, in heavy rain or intensely hot sun, moving down stretches of road past fields with dark chemical fertilizer that smelled so badly I got a headache from it. Most days our feet were sore and tired although compared to some pilgrims' foot problems, we did not experience any of their difficulties. One pilgrim's bunions prevented her from wearing hiking boots. She slipped her often bloody, bandaged feet into sandals every day, walking on the sharp stones and gullies full of rocks. How she managed that "feat of feet" is beyond me.

When the day's walking ended, we hand washed our clothes. This was not a difficulty, just a nuisance, but on a few occasions it brought with it some of its own problems, like the time we hung our wash on clotheslines directly above caked, red soil. While we were away for our evening meal the wind and rain came, blowing our clothes into the dirt, creating a real mess. Although it was well after sundown, we washed everything again and hung it on our bunk beds in hopes of drying. The clothes were still wet in the morning so we pinned our wet underwear and shirts to our back-packs as we walked along in the sun.

When we were at Grañón, we hung our wet clothes to dry on lines in a dark, dusty church belfry full of spider webs. I found it hard to locate the narrow door leading to that creepy place. Once inside, the grey light made it equally difficult to find the door to get out. I thought of yelling for help but doubted anyone could hear me. I was in there alone and panicked when at first I couldn't find the exit.

Washing always held a bit of challenge. In Eirexe, one of the pilgrims washed everything except what she was wearing. She hung her wash on a clothesline across the road. Later on, a local farmer herded his cows right past the lines and, of course, the cows brushed her newly washed items with their muddy, fly-covered bodies.

Eventually I saw the worth in the small, irritating difficulties. I would not have chosen any of the troubles we encountered on the Camino but, in looking back, the lessons are clear. No matter what the size of the problem, each one offered an opportunity to perceive life in a more universal context and to acknowledge the privileged life I have.

The food issue brought me into communion with the larger world. One evening as we waited hungrily for the restaurants to open at 8:00 p.m. so we could have our dinner, I wrote:

I am so hungry. For all the walking today we ate little: bread and coffee, day-old bacon and cheese sandwich, apple and nectarine and some nuts. That's all. I think I need to learn to be hungry and to eat less. All these indigenous people who walk so far to work every day. They eat very little. I can unite with them and join with the many people who have little to eat.

A related teaching came from the lack of privacy. Every pilgrim was in the same situation in the refugios. Knowing each of us faced a similar challenge strengthened my sense of oneness.

Lack of privacy also helped to lessen the strong hold I have on individuality and protective, private space. I grew in awareness of the millions of people on the planet who do not have the luxury of space and privacy I have at home. It was good to enter a world where this luxury was lacking. It honed and sharpened my sense of compassion.

Dim lighting, limited water for showers, and no toilet paper allowed me to conserve these vital sources of our planet that are used carelessly and thoughtlessly by most Americans, including myself. The experience of doing without what I consider to be essential encourages me to safeguard and carefully use the planet's natural resources.

The strong teaching of the Camino's difficulties can be found in this note I wrote to myself when I was trying to make sense out of the daily challenges:

> *Perhaps we will come full circle and return home with relish to what seemed ho-hum to us before. Today Tom spoke of how much he'd love to be in his comfortable chair, retired, doing nothing, and thoroughly enjoying it. Yes, me, too. Perhaps I will return to my work with a greater sense of appreciation for what I have moaned and groaned about in the past. Now the thought of basic creature comforts is strong in me. I hope I never forget how little I had of those comforts while on the road.*

The boulder-like, insurmountable difficulty with which I struggled all through the Camino was bathroom dirt. I heard myself complaining and whining about grimy restrooms anytime I encountered them. What the Camino taught me through this lack of acceptance is that when I focus on a tough situation and allow it to take over my mind and emotions, this resistance deters and overpowers the other good things which I easily miss. When I obsessed about the dirt of a refugio, I quickly forgot the joy and bounty of being on the pilgrimage as well as the blessing of having a nightly place of shelter. The problem of dirt taught me to acknowledge difficult things but not to allow myself to be overly preoccupied with them.

EACH OF THE CAMINO's difficulties brought an awareness, a challenge to grow and a call to be grateful. A year later, I am still conscious of what I did not have on the Camino when I step into a clean bathroom, sit down to a meal with foods of my choice, sink into a soft chair, and wiggle my feet without sensing any soreness. I sigh with immense contentment, remembering the days when I was dealing with the Camino's pebbles and boulders.

11

EMBRACE BEAUTY

In bleak and difficult times
you must always keep something beautiful
in your heart.

—Pascal

Beauty sustains me in challenging times. This was never more true than when I walked the Camino. The pilgrimage was far from being a "bleak" time but the arduous and challenging nature of it required my heart to sip daily of beauty's strength. Intuitive wisdom surely guided those who first established the route now designated as the traditional pilgrimage to Santiago de Compostela. The choice of the territory across northern Spain with its diverse and immeasurably beautiful landscape provides what one needs for inner equilibrium. This beauty balances the physical demands of endless miles of walking. Coming down every hill, turning every corner on the Camino, there is always something new and lovely to bless the eye and heart.

Beauty was everywhere: layers of misty mountains, voices and faces of villagers, olive groves, proud roosters announcing dawn, cathedral spires praising the skies, medieval bridges waiting to be crossed, cowbells tingling and clanging in meadows, tall white propellers of wind farms, eucalyptus trees, winding rivers, comforting views of villages below high hills, and endless patches of enticing grains, vegetables, and fruits of all sorts including succulent, wild blackberries.

Beauty consoled and strengthened me during the countless times my legs and feet hurt from walking and my shoulders pained from carrying my backpack. The Camino's loveliness uplifted me when my body sagged from illness. Beauty brought back contentment when I whined about unsanitary bathroom conditions. The natural splendor around me gave me hope when my hungry soul longed for a touch of enthusiasm. Always the many forms of beauty on the Camino reached out to me, asking nothing more than that I embrace their gifts.

I wasn't expecting the beauty I found. Tom and I began the Camino on the heels of one of Spain's hottest summers ever. Newscasts told of the grape harvest in France coming earlier than usual. I doubted we would see much of Spain's flowering and fruitful attractiveness by the time we arrived in early September. I expected the landscape to be brown, dry, and brittle. How wrong I was.

What a surprise I received the first day when my senses filled with the green of conifers and the forest's moist scent. As we made our way down the Pyrenees, my spirit danced when I beheld countless patches of flowers etching the path and dotting the meadows. Color burst forth, alive and bountiful, not dead and dormant as I had expected. This beauty urged me onward. As we moved beyond it, through the flower-filled parks of Pamplona, and into the wide fields of the rural area, my heart leapt to see vineyards heavily laden with luscious purple and green grapes. Day after day, mile after mile, I found myself immersed in loveliness, never tiring of the fertile vineyards' companionship.

Except for the beauty of the verdant green hills and ancient oak trees in Galicia, nothing brought me such pleasure and sustenance as the endless fields of grapevines. For days the vineyards bordered us on both sides. I sometimes stopped to gaze with pleasure at the healthy green vines laden with their abundant harvest. Whenever I did so, Tom would say, "I have something to read to you but I think it's not quite the right time." He kept teasing me with this message until we came one day to an absolutely astounding view of a vineyard near Ventosa. "Stop!" he exclaimed. "This is it! I've been waiting to come to the most beautiful spot to read something I carried with me from home."

He then proceeded to dramatically pull out a tiny slip of paper from his pocket. As the two of us stood there side by side in the hot sun, facing bejeweled hillsides filled with ripened clusters of burgundy grapes, he read this poem to me:

> *Back of the vines is the vintner,*
> *and back through the years his skill,*
> *and back of it all are the vines in the sun,*
> *and the rain and the Master's will.*

I do not know who authored that poem but when Tom read it to me my heart melted into oneness with the grapes, the blue sky, the soil, the sunshine, our friendship, and the Creator. Tom's little poem was a great reminder that beauty is a central source of connection with the sacred. We remained there in quiet awe on our ninth day of walking. In that moment every piece of beauty from the past eight days on the Camino quietly bonded me with a much greater Beauty. Tom and I both stood there peacefully smiling, silently sensing the communion we felt with God, with one another, and with the harvest before us. Three days later I wrote in my journal:

> *I know there will be tough times ahead but all the beauty I have seen, the great people I've met already, all of this assures me that God is with me. And that I am meant to travel this path.*

"Beauty is a celebration of is-ness" writes JoAnne Dodgson, author of *Gifts of the Grandmother*. She emphasizes how beauty resides within every moment: "Beauty is felt here in the now, with no if-only's or should-be's or someday-it-might-be's." How right her observation is but I needed the Camino's beauty to bring me back to that reality. It leapt out at me and stood me upright in the middle of the "is-ness." There is no way to sidestep the Camino's abundant beauty.

On one particular day, the path led us through vegetable farms and orchards, with distant mountain ranges on either side of us. We walked past rows and rows of tall asparagus plants, a sunflower field, apple orchards, walnut and almond groves. To our right a farmer created striking patterns as he plowed a harvested field on a rolling hillside. We even spied a stork in a huge nest that overflowed a tall, thin, circular chimney. Walking in the midst of this ordinary beauty, moving amid all that "is-ness," created a magical, mystical mood. It was revitalizing. I thought: "All I need is beauty to keep my heart alive and all beauty needs is my attention."

Each time I was sure I had seen the best of northern Spain's beauty another region opened up with new vistas and vegetation. My spirit soared as we left Astorga for the walk toward the mountains in the region of Galicia. We had traveled the 150 miles of the mesa's flatlands for many days. As we left the dry heat behind us, I felt the soft air ease and moisten my thirsty skin. More and more green appeared with every mile. Birds regularly serenaded us after their near-silence on the mesa. Scrub oaks, pine, a type of mesquite, juniper, lots of bushes of lavender, heather, rosemary, and fennel covered the hillsides along the path. Layers of purple and blue mountains in the distance beckoned us forward.

I loved the "new face" of the walk that appeared every day. As we hiked down a steep hill glorious flowers appeared: roses, hibiscus, fuchsia, gladiola, and lupine. I often paused to smell them. My knees creaked from the sharp descent but the fragrance of the flowers eased the pain. That day we saw two small mule deer. They leapt across the path and up the verdant hillside. Spotting the first wildlife on the Camino thrilled us. The following week we sighted a fox as he ran across the path amid chestnut trees and poplars. (Other than that, we viewed few wild animals on the Camino.)

Sometimes beauty was hidden. In O Cebreiro, when I was fatigued and impatient with the day's tough route, I noted the elusiveness of beauty. The day was terribly foggy. We were soaked from rain and exhausted from the strenuous climb. I was annoyed with the overpriced lunch at the local café where we waited for the refugio to open. I wanted to collapse on a bunk bed. As we waited in the café, the thick fog instantly lifted and a bright sun beamed on the hilly terrain. Everyone inside the café ran to the windows and gasped together as the vista opened up for us. Intense green covered the continuous stretch of hills and valleys. Cows and sheep serenely grazed on neatly sectioned farmland. It was simply magnificent. I couldn't help but notice the gift this beauty bestowed: a swift mood change and a lessening of my weariness.

Usually the Camino's beauty was obvious. There was truly never a place that lacked beauty of some form. Each day was like stepping into a splendid art gallery. Some of the best views came near the end when we walked toward Arca. The trail constantly took us through dense woods filled with old oak trees. In that area we walked through what I called "the tunnels." These open paths went through the woods but they were sometimes below the level of the land, near the base of tree trunks. In these earthen, wide, roofless tunnels were ivy, moss, and the pungent odor of soil. These cool, shaded "tunnels" with the umbrella of tree foliage above us extended for miles. As we embraced this beauty, the beauty embraced us. All day I felt as though I was in an earthen cathedral. The path evoked exquisite reverence. Conversation ceased as the surrounding beauty united us to a sacred presence.

I ALSO FOUND BEAUTY in the rain. Of the thirty-seven days we walked the Camino, during at least two weeks the weather included some form of moisture, either mist, light rainfall, or steady showers. Except for heavy downpours, I found more blessing than burden in the rain. The forests and farmlands reached for the wetness. I could almost hear the soil and vegetation sighing with relief after the heat they endured. Those moist days held a stillness and a comforting gentleness. Their wetness wrapped soft arms around my weariness and refreshed me.

One night a great rain storm pounded the refugio with wild winds. As we left the next morning, I dreaded having to plod through the mud that awaited us on the trail. Once we were on our way, I soon changed my focus from mud to fresh air and the sparkle of raindrops. It was one of the most gorgeous days we walked. The wild winds of the storm moved the heat and humidity out and left us with a strong, brilliantly blue sky. I was inspired and refreshed with the beauty we saw and in spite of my physical fatigue, a new eagerness for the pilgrimage sang in me. Even the tall grasses of the meadows whispered enthusiasm that day.

I loved best of all the mornings we started out in the dark. On those days we walked silently under the stars, with the countryside serenely quiet before dawn. Gradually, the first bird began to sing. Eventually, as light seeped into the darkness, we turned around from time to time so we could catch the rising sun. Sometimes we stopped and stood in awe as daybreak spread color across the eastern horizon. One early dawn we were awestruck as we walked between the two companions of our planet: the red ball of sun rising over our shoulder though thick mist in the east and the full moon hanging elegantly before us in the west. I couldn't imagine wanting to be any other place at that moment. As my heart embraced the dawn, I noticed how beauty strengthened us—our morning stride, sometimes sleepy and slow, was steady and strong.

Beauty on the Camino revealed itself in more than the glory of a sunrise and the layers of misted mountains. Sometimes we found it in the simplest of places like the old shed near the edge of La Laguana in the region of Galicia. Tom and I had walked uphill in the rain for several hours so we stopped to rest and eat a snack. Sheltered from the rain, we sat on a scratchy bale of hay, amid the smell of farm machinery and animals, with the sound of rain pattering on the roof. How could it be beautiful? It was. The color of the straw, the shelter from the downpour, the music of the raindrops, the gift of a friend, together these things brought ease and a moment of contentment to both spirit and body. When we rose from the bale of hay to continue our walk through the rest of the steep hills, I found renewed zest in my heart.

While beauty embraced me through nature, it also reached out to me in the medieval bridges and the lovely cathedrals. When I sat in the exquisite thirteenth-century cathedral of León with its hundred stained-glass windows, I felt like I was in the center of a kaleidoscope. Similarly, when I gazed at the cathedral of Burgos with its many Gothic spires, I stood in awe of the beauty human hands create.

Individuals as well as groups filled the Camino with another kind of beauty. Never a day went by without our encountering the wonder of humanity. Farm families herded cows through the village to milking sites and then back out to pasture. An entrepreneurial woman stood by her house selling warm crepes. An old shepherd with a bad limp tended his sheep. Families streamed out of their homes after siesta to meet for leisure and meals in Burgos where both the elderly in wheelchairs and fresh babies in buggies were pushed up and down the wide, tree-canopied Paseo along the Arlonzon River. A young waitress who was a psychology and English major laughed heartily with Tom and me as she tried out her command of the English language while we dined.

I found beauty in people's faces and in the simple, joyful way the rural people celebrated. They brought happiness and laughter with them. We arrived in one village on the weekend of a huge harvest fiesta. From a long distance we heard church bells ringing. When we arrived, a loud, raucous band consisting of three saxophones, three trumpets, two drums, and two cymbals played in the plaza. Young girls and boys (all ages to mid-teens) and a few adults filled buckets, bottles, and other containers with water from a large fountain and profusely doused each other. Then they linked arms, two to six persons across, and danced in a walking or stomping step around and around the plaza. Laughter and conversation came from the bars where men, women, and children gathered to eat, drink, and celebrate the harvest. The band went around to every part of the town and played all afternoon.

Music was something I missed immensely while walking on the Camino. I thirsted for the harmony that music offered to my spirit. There were only three or four refugios that provided music. In several this consisted of songs for evening prayer. In Puente la Reina, baroque music wafted through the building. In Ruitelán, two Buddhist directors, Mañuel and José, sent a marvelous rendition of "Ave Maria" through the house to awaken us in the morning. Each time I heard music of any kind my heart leapt.

Beautiful music, even snatches of it, lightened my spirit. On the 30th of September we stopped in the Ponferrada basilica and heard taped classical music playing. I sat there indulging my ears and heart and struggled when it was time to get up and leave. I longed for music because its beauty restored my body and spirit almost as much as a good night's rest. Music brought tears to my eyes for a third time on the Camino when the opening song for the pilgrim Mass at the cathedral in Santiago was one of the three Spanish songs Tom and I sang every day: "Vienen con Alegria— We Come with Joy." That song, and the closing one of "Salve Regina," my religious community's "theme song," touched me deeply.

There was one other time on the Camino where the beauty of music literally lifted me off my feet. On September 28th after we walked about three miles, we came across the old abandoned town of Foncebadón. This place is being restored and now a few people live there. A bar was open and the sounds of Gaelic music inside escaped out the windows. Even though I had my backpack strapped on, I started to step merrily to the rhythm as we approached the place. I danced through the door into the bar and kept on tapping my feet the whole time, unable to keep my body or my spirit still. Once again, beauty reached out to me. This time I couldn't help but embrace it and when I did, a flood of new energy arose within me.

Beauty awakens what is sleeping in our spirit. It relieves the veins of tiredness and stirs up what lays dormant in an over-emphasis on activity. We all too easily lose our connection with the world's splendor in our attempt to meet each day's demands on our time and energy. Beauty lifts the veil from the treasures of our heart that we quickly discard in our fast-paced world. The loveliness of life restores and regenerates our enthusiasm by its "is-ness." When we embrace beauty we come home to that part of our self that cries out for nurturance and renewal.

I FIND IT IMPOSSIBLE to describe all the beauty I experienced on the Camino. To do so would fill a book by itself. Even as I write about it, my heart grows large and full in remembrance. Beauty does that to us. It revisits us with joy, calls to us with its lucidity and strength, and unites us over and over to the deeper thread of the holy within us and among us. Each visitation of beauty, whether newly experienced or reclaimed in memory, can help us believe in life's goodness.

The Camino's beauty strengthened my soul. It restored my attentiveness and reminded me not to miss its blessedness. Wherever I am, I never have to look far for this beauty. Always beauty awaits me. All it needs is my awareness and my embrace. Each of us needs to hold something beautiful in our heart.

12

EXPERIENCE HOMELESSNESS

I had occasion to visit the city shelter last month
where homeless families are cared for.
I sat there for a couple of hours,
contemplating poverty and destitution.

—*Dorothy Day*

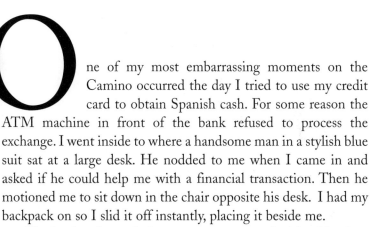

ne of my most embarrassing moments on the Camino occurred the day I tried to use my credit card to obtain Spanish cash. For some reason the ATM machine in front of the bank refused to process the exchange. I went inside to where a handsome man in a stylish blue suit sat at a large desk. He nodded to me when I came in and asked if he could help me with a financial transaction. Then he motioned me to sit down in the chair opposite his desk. I had my backpack on so I slid it off instantly, placing it beside me.

The banker first asked to see my passport for identification. Wouldn't you know, the passport lay at the bottom of my pack. I stood up and began digging around to find the precious item. At that moment I regretted hiding my passport underneath everything for fear of it being stolen. I stretched my short arm inside my pack and struggled to reach around things in order to get way down to the bottom. Impossible. I embarrassingly took some of my items out in order to reach the passport. As I did so, a strong aroma wafted into the room. Goat cheese! I forgot it was in my pack. This provision was great to carry because of its hard texture and durability. Goat cheese also had a very distinct odor which I paid little attention to it until I stood before the banker. Oh, how pungent that cheese smelled!

My face became redder and redder as I kept searching for the passport. Finally, my hand touched it and I sighed with relief. As I looked up to hand it to the banker I saw a pasted, thin smile on his dark, lean face. He appeared patient but I spied a bit of disdain. "Hummm," I thought, "he probably wants to hold his nose." I apologized to the banker and again he gave me that silent, pasted smile. There was no doubt in my mind his brain was storing up the scene to retell at the dinner table that night: "This smelly pilgrim with her dirty hiking boots dug into this pack of weird things and, whew, the odor that came from that bag, it was enough to gag me. . . . "

After the banker assisted me with the transaction and politely bid me farewell, I took my pack and walked out the door. I don't know which of us felt more relieved at my departure. As I stood outside on the sidewalk and restored my passport to the bottom of my pack, I had this powerful insight: "I am like a homeless person. This is how people back home see and smell them." Until that morning, I had not tuned into homeless people's humiliation or the superior attitudes hovering over them.

The bank incident preceded several other situations in which I experienced a tiny bit of what it is to be a homeless person. At certain times I felt terribly out of place and inappropriately dressed in my pilgrim attire. I rarely thought of how I was clad or what I looked like except when we walked through large cities and mingled with people wearing lovely clothes. I did not have any "nice clothes" to wear. Around well-dressed people, I looked and felt grubby. Although I showered and washed my clothes by hand at the end of each day's walk, inevitably I looked grimy and smelled a bit grungy when I met someone, especially by later afternoon. I perspired in the hot sun, walked through cow and sheep manure, and stirred up dust on unpaved roads. No wonder I appeared disheveled and smelled slightly offensive.

One Sunday afternoon we walked into Villalcázar de Sirga, site of the impressive, thirteenth-century church of Santa María la Blanca, a historical building of the Knights Templar who guarded the Camino in the Middle Ages. The streets were packed with cars because of a wedding in the church. Tom and I did not know the location of the refugio or what time it opened. He went to search out information on housing while I found a spot across from the church to stand and watch his backpack. As I stood there, I leaned back on the wall outside a restaurant.

No sooner did I position myself when customers dressed in their wedding fineries stepped out to depart the restaurant. In no time at all, I realized I was standing in the wrong place. The people cast their glances on me with scowls and dirty looks, as if to say, "Why are you here, you repugnant woman? Go someplace else!" I suppose I did appear a bit out of place with my hiking shorts, dirty boots, lopsided sunhat, and bulging backpack. Still, I did no harm as I stood there waiting. Their disdainful looks pierced me with rejection. Immediately, I thought about homeless folks receiving those same looks much of the time.

On another occasion when Tom and I completed a long day's walk, we looked and smelled anything but pleasant. We needed food for the next day so we went to shop before settling into the refugio. Because of our weariness, we chose to save our energy by not taking our packs off and setting them down outside the store. Instead, we walked into the store wearing them. Soon after we were inside, a store clerk followed me up and down the aisles. At first, I naively presumed she wanted to help me find what I needed. I turned and greeted her with "Hola" but she responded with a glaring, suspicious look. I was stunned. Then I knew she was following me because she thought I might steal something. I guess I looked "the type" to do so.

The longer I walked on the Camino the more my awareness of the destitute increased. I often felt this way when Tom and I were concerned about finding housing for the evening. We never knew for sure if we would have a roof over our heads or not. Even though money was not a problem, housing locations could be full, or there might not even be a refugio, a hostel, or a hotel in which to stay. Sometimes we consoled ourselves by saying, "We can always knock on someone's door and ask to sleep in their garage," or "We can find a park and sleep there." I did meet one pilgrim who slept mostly on church doorsteps or in parks as he walked the Camino. More than once I thought to myself, "What must it be like for a person on the street to try to find shelter for the night?"

Waiting in line for refugios to open gave me a sense of how the homeless wait in line at soup kitchens and at shelters. Like them, Tom and I stepped into conditions we could not control once the doors opened. These conditions included dim lighting, sometimes one lone light bulb of 35 watts hanging without a shade in the middle of a room of thirty people, or stairwells and toilet areas with no lighting at all. Like the homeless, we felt relieved to have a roof over our heads even if it meant cramped space in dormitories with dense air, dirty conditions, and grungy mattresses. When we found housing at Portomarín I wrote:

> *Staying at a municipal refugio. I am sitting on the top bunk, on my sleeping bag, which is on a mattress with a dirty, torn cover. The foam shows through the large rip. There are feathers from the pillow and particles of dirt on the foam and on the mattress cover. On my right, there is a two-pane window. It's filthy. The inside has mud-caked dirt around it. The panes are all smudged and blackened with fly specks. In this room there are 5 bunk beds all situated around the walls, leaving the center with a narrow row of free space.*

> *Outside my window, pilgrims sit at the entrance to the refugio, speaking in various languages. They are sitting on an old stone wall that parallels the entrance. I despise these huge, filthy places. I did not take a shower, just cleaned up a little bit. There is only cold water, two showers that are wide open, two sinks, two toilets. No paper and the floor is totally wet and muddy.*

Along with the conditions of the refugios we stayed in, we also experienced sleeping in a different place almost every night. Each day we unpacked and repacked, putting each item in its plastic bag and making sure we put everything in the best place for carrying. We did not stay long enough to become familiar with a place. Each night we learned a new route to the toilet and adjusted our body to a different bed.

Special attempts to be kind to us also cost us a bit of our dignity. When we arrived at Arzúa the refugio director led us up to the third floor to where single cots, not bunk beds, lined the room. When I looked into the room, I felt overjoyed until I noticed a white piece of paper lying on the beds with the printed message: *gente mayor* (old people). The beds were reserved for elderly pilgrims and the director considered me to be one of them!

Washing clothes also linked me to the homeless. I have often heard refined people remark about the poor, "Well, at least they could look clean." Being clean is not so easy as one imagines. First, we sought the sink designated for washing clothes, waited in line to use it, hoped our soap lasted, hurried so another pilgrim could step forward and begin. Next, we looked for the designated place to hang our clothes to dry. When many pilgrims stayed in the refugio and there were only a few clotheslines, or sometimes none at all, we hung our washing on bushes and fences and anyplace that held wet clothes. I can't begin to tell you how excited we felt the two or three times we stayed at a refugio that had a washing machine. One even included a clothes dryer. What a joy to have clothes that really felt clean.

Food offered another opportunity to associate my experience with that of the homeless. I never knew hunger the way I knew it on the Camino. Several times we ran out of food and could get nothing to eat for miles. Even when food was readily available it was not always something of our choice. On the fourth night of our trek, on a Sunday, we stopped at Cizur Menor, a little way beyond Pamplona. Until time for the evening meal, we did not know most eating places in Spain close on Sundays. There was nothing open in Cizur Menor. A few places might have been open in Pamplona but that meant walking a long distance back into the city and hunting for one. The owner of the private refugio gave us an option of ordering food from a delivery place that remained open in

Pamplona. We chose the delivered food after Tom exclaimed excitedly, "Hey, pizza! Let's go for it!" Our mouths salivated with the thought of food different from the usual pilgrim fare. We felt famished by the time the pizza arrived an hour or so later.

When we sat down to eat the pizza, I could hardly take more than a few bites. That pizza was the worst food on the Camino. Even Tom, who always insisted he "could eat anything," was unable to stomach the stuff. We chose not to eat the foul tasting food and couldn't even give it away to other hungry pilgrims! No one wanted it. That experience, and the many days when we waited hours for restaurants to open after a long day's walk, caused me to ask Tom, "How do the indigenous do it—going without food after working hard all day? How do the homeless manage to eat whatever is given to them even when it tastes awful?"

The refugios provided breakfast once in awhile, which was a special gift because we did not use food from our packs and could save it for later in the day. These breakfasts were mostly white bread left over from dinner the night before. We felt grateful for whatever food the refugios offered but we were absolutely elated when fresh fruit or an occasional yogurt or cereal showed up on the dining table in the morning.

Those of us who have access to any and all kinds of food may think hungry people are lucky to have any food at all. In a way, I suppose this is true, but what a pleasure to bite into something delicious, to relish a food that our taste buds enjoy. How wonderful to have food that is not just filling but also nourishing and healthy. Everyone ought to have the option of this enjoyment.

Several months after returning home, I read an article in *The Des Moines Register* about a local church that provided a fish fry at a shelter. Several church members saved their summer's catch and wanted to share it with the homeless. The people on the streets who gathered for the meal raved about how good it tasted. After the easy-to-prepare-and-serve, starchy, thick casserole-type foods usually served, the fish dinner was a banquet for them. One homeless man remarked gratefully, "It's the first time I've eaten fish in two years." Had I not been on the Camino, his comment would have held less meaning for me.

My sparse belongings on the Camino also connected me to the homeless. I guarded my few simple possessions like they were gold, not so much out of fear they would be stolen by other pilgrims but because I didn't want to be without one of my precious items. Each one was vital to my journey. When I lived among the disenfranchised two summers in Appalachia, several times I observed the poor sharing what little they had to help another person in need. On the Camino, I also experienced this generosity. One night when Tom and I initially thought we would have nothing to eat for the evening meal, an eighty-year-old Canadian named Philip offered Tom and me all his food. He insisted we take the half loaf of bread and small chunk of cheese he held out to us, saying, "It's okay. I'm not hungry. I had a big lunch." His gesture of generosity touched me deeply because I knew he must be hungry, too. As it turned out, we found food that evening for all of us but had we not, Philip was willing to give of the little he had. (By the way, Philip ate a huge helping of everything at dinner that evening.)

Late in our journey, Tom turned to me and said, "If I had to describe each day of the Camino, I'd name it 'how to survive' day: how to take care of our body, how to feed and house ourselves, how to keep ourselves clean." He pointed out that pilgrims, like the homeless, experience a daily challenge to have their basic needs of life met. I agreed but I also recognized how different our journey was from that of the homeless. Tom and I deliberately chose to eat the simple pilgrim meal at bars and restaurants. We chose to dress as we did and we chose to stay in the refugios. Choice is rarely possible for those who have no money, no job, no home.

OUR PILGRIMAGE GIFTED US with only a brief glimpse of the homeless. I do not intend, in any way, to romanticize our Camino experience as I compare it to that of being homeless. The two situations are not the same. However, the Camino did provide a keen awareness and a renewed compassion for the plight of those who live from day to day, who do not know where the next meal or the night's housing will be. The Camino was never a "game" to me. I felt the hunger. I loathed the dirt. I sensed the rejection. Yet, I knew my situation to be only temporary. I knew I could leave the Camino and return to everything the homeless do not have.

This lesson of the pilgrimage continues to provide reflection on my attitude toward undocumented immigrants, homeless wanderers, and all those who are disenfranchised. Not long after my return home, I attended a meeting in downtown Des Moines. As I placed coins in the meter, an unshaven, dirt-encrusted, homeless man with his bundle of belongings passed by me. Normally, I'd have averted my gaze. This time I looked directly into his eyes, smiled, and greeted him with, "Good morning." The homeless man looked surprised by my greeting him as another human being. He grunted a "hi" in return and went on his way. Little did he know how much kinship I felt at that moment.

When Christmas came two months after our return from the Camino, both Tom and I confessed to feeling depressed with the largess of gift-giving and the contrast between the life we experienced on the Camino and the life to which we returned. As we pondered this reality, I realized I was approaching life in a new way. The Camino opened my heart more fully to those who seek the basics of life. I can no longer turn away. I want to remember always their right to have the essentials of life that I have.

The first Christmas after walking the Camino, I decided to buy fewer gifts for those who already had more than they needed. The money I saved went to food pantries and shelters for the homeless. I continue to do this in memory of all those who extended kindness when I walked the long route to Santiago, all those who took me in and offered me a place in their compassion.

I will not forget my own sense of homelessness on the Camino. I want it to influence me forever.

13

RETURN A POSITIVE
FOR A NEGATIVE

To let go of judgment does not mean that you don't see what they do. It means that you recognize their behavior as a form of conditioning, and you see it and accept it as that. You don't construct an identity out of it for that person.

—*Eckhart Tolle*

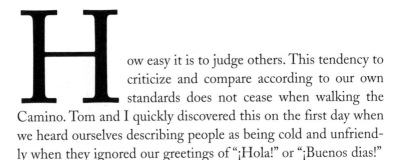

ow easy it is to judge others. This tendency to criticize and compare according to our own standards does not cease when walking the Camino. Tom and I quickly discovered this on the first day when we heard ourselves describing people as being cold and unfriendly when they ignored our greetings of "¡Hola!" or "¡Buenos dias!"

On the following day, Tom mused, "Isn't it something? We call out a positive greeting of hello and then we follow it quickly with a harsh comment about them if they don't greet us in return. That negativity destroys the good we hope to do by our greeting. Besides, why do we expect everyone here to say 'hello' to us in return? In the United States we do not say 'hello' to everyone we pass. It would wear us out."

We decided to make a strong effort to have a more positive approach when we met others, no matter how they looked or acted. This decision called us to replace a negative thought or feeling with a positive one. Whenever one or the other of us spoke about someone unfavorably we tried to replace it with something affirming. Our desire to do this stemmed partly from the tenet of our Christian faith to love others. Our decision also came from our mutual belief that it takes more energy to think and speak negatively than it does to think and speak positively. From then on, we encouraged good energy and love to go into our thinking and responding. This goal challenged us.

The first huge lesson about not judging others came when we walked through Pamplona. After Tom and I walked several hours through the city we both needed a restroom but it was Sunday and we could not find one open. The public toilets in the parks were closed as well as stores and restaurants. Both of us grew increasingly anxious by the time we neared the other side of the city. Then we came upon a sign pointing to the University of Pamplona. "Ah," I said with great relief, "surely there are some toilets in one of the buildings there" and we headed in that direction.

Up the hill from our walk, we saw three priests in black suits and Roman collars. We thought they might be Jesuits. They were loading suitcases into a car next to a large stone building on the university campus, obviously preparing to depart for a trip. We hurried up the pathway to ask them about a restroom. The priests immediately stopped packing the car and escorted us through an elegantly decorated entryway into the building. I felt out of place with my wet boots and shabby pilgrim clothes but the three seemed not to mind as they showed Tom and me to separate restrooms. I was thrilled with the beauty of the marble walls and the sparkling cleanliness after my stays in soiled refugios. The restroom even had toilet paper and hand soap! The priests waited for us and then offered to show us their beautiful chapel. Tom and I stood outside with them afterward where they conversed warmly with us.

Tom asked them if they were Jesuits. "Oh, no," one of them replied in surprise, "we belong to Opus Dei." Another priest quickly added, "We are canon lawyers and ethics professors at this university of 1,000 students." I was stunned. My mind yelled "Opus Dei!" as I tried to take in the information. I couldn't believe it. I didn't dare look at Tom to see what his reaction was. I knew he had to be as shocked as I was. We both knew Opus Dei to be an extremely conservative, wealthy, Catholic organization with strong ties to traditional circles in Rome. Although Tom and I were a Catholic priest and sister, neither of us had much in common with this group. Yet, there we were, graciously received by these three priests who were kind enough to stop their own activities to attend pilgrims in need.

After we bid the Opus Dei priests farewell and continued on our walk, Tom and I chuckled at our error of thinking them to be Jesuits. We turned our attention, then, to the kindness of the priests. Both of us were touched by their welcome. It mattered not whether the three were conservative or liberal. They reached out to us with warmth and care, offering us Christian hospitality. In this regard we had a common purpose with them, for Tom and I also believed wholeheartedly in extending hospitality to others.

Tom and I couldn't stop marveling at what we had experienced. The event was a powerful lesson about nonjudgment. The priests' kindness taught us to remember we are all human beings who happen to have differing views about such things as theology. As we continued to talk about the unfair judgments we tend to make, Tom mused, "Why do we focus first on what separates us, like liberal or conservative? Why don't we approach what first connects us, like the fact we are all children of one God, all temples of one Spirit? That's the bond we have. That's what matters."

Receiving the kindness of the Opus Dei priests created an opportune moment of strengthening our resolve to set aside negative thoughts and attitudes for positive ones. As the weeks went by on the Camino, we became increasingly conscious of how our minds slid into negative judgments. Fortunately, what bothered Tom usually did not bother me and vice versa so we caught our negativity rather swiftly when one or the other of us started making judgmental comments.

Not a day went by without our having to exchange a positive for a negative. We struggled not to make negative comments about others who were walking the Camino. Pilgrims are a diverse group. The temptation is to judge what they wear and eat, what they believe or don't believe, and how they speak and act. A good portion of negative judgments are eliminated by remembering each pilgrim brings his or her own personality and history to the Camino. Tom and I developed the practice of thinking about each pilgrim as "a story."

When they stepped onto the Camino, pilgrims brought their own identity, the life narrative that shaped and formed them, just as we brought our own individuality. Meister Eckhart wrote: *"Every creature is a book about God."* When Tom and I remembered this, we withheld negative judgments of other pilgrims—but we often forgot.

When I observed certain pilgrim behavior which I considered selfish or immature, negative thoughts came leaping up in me like frisky frogs. One morning I observed a young lad sitting sideways, blocking the stair steps in the morning as he greased his toes. I felt irritated with him as I came down the steps and he did not move aside. Every pilgrim stepped over his legs to get downstairs. I wondered how I could turn my negative response to him into a positive one. Then I thought of his age. He was probably half awake early in the morning and completely unaware of the problem he was causing. This positive thought erased my irritation toward the youth.

SOME SITUATIONS REQUIRED a bit more searching for a positive to offset a negative. An older pilgrim sat alone working a crossword puzzle at one of two tables outside the only bar in a little village and never once invited the seven or eight tired pilgrims standing nearby to share the table. Again, I tried to observe rather than judge her actions. I thought, "Her own life story is somehow here in her actions. Like her, I have taken myself on this Camino. All my own warts and shadow stuff show up and cause unease for others. I cannot judge this woman for what she is doing."

A few days later, when I saw a careless pilgrim washing his clothes in a drinking fountain I was horrified. After all it was the place where pilgrims came to fill their water bottles. I was so upset I almost went over and told him to stop. Not until the next day did I remember how four of us pilgrims had stopped and washed our muddy boots off in a similar water source for pilgrims at Villamayor Monjardín several weeks earlier. That memory put a quick halt on my negative thoughts about *the careless pilgrim* I had judged so severely.

Just about the time Tom and I thought we had our negative thinking licked, it started up again. One night a German couple moved into the bunk beds opposite us. The woman was speaking tearfully to her husband. She was a blonde in her fifties, well dressed in expensive sports clothes, and had a lot of gold jewelry. I reflected, "I don't suppose this is her idea of fun." Then I checked my negativity and tried to replace it with a positive: "I'm not a classy woman like her but I, too, understand how hard it is to accept this style of living. How tough it must be for her." Later on, I discovered she was in great physical pain from a bad fall she took in the rain. Her twisted knee was the actual cause of her crying, not the condition of the refugio. How wrongly I had judged her.

A similar false judgment happened with Tom. When we met our Canadian named Philip, he told us he was eighty years old. We enjoyed him a lot. Some days later we were in a refugio and Tom noticed Philip had registered the night before listing his age as seventy-seven. The age difference was insignificant to me but for some unknown reason, Tom felt chagrined about that discrepancy and thought Philip to be dishonest. Imagine Tom's embarrassment when he found out two days later that the Philip in the register was actually another Canadian with the same name who really was seventy-seven years old.

The two of us experienced yet another situation in which we learned not to make judgments about others. One of the groups Tom struggled to appreciate involved a little band of French folks who walked together. Each morning a van dropped this group with small daypacks off and at night picked them up and took them to a place for dinner. The French pilgrims often stayed in the same refugios as Tom and I. The group was a noisy lot, talking and having a good time. This constant chattering and noisiness irritated Tom. Every once in awhile, he talked to me about wanting to overcome his feelings about "the French group."

This pilgrim group ended up helping Tom with his negativity when we walked into Burgos. Tom and I reached the sleazy area of the city when we heard excited voices. As we looked over, the French pilgrims motioned for us to come across the busy four-lane street. The two of us hesitated. We were following the Camino's yellow arrows and felt we were headed in the right direction, but we decided to go over and see what the French wanted. When we reached the pilgrims one of them explained, "Our guidebook warns pilgrims to be very careful of pickpockets and muggers who prey on pilgrims in this part of town." They expressed concern for us and urged us to take the bus with them to the heart of the city, which we did.

Tom and I often talked about our efforts to return a positive for a negative. One day I wrote in my journal:

> *Tom and I have had a talk about negative thinking. We want to send only positive thoughts, to eliminate negative thinking from our minds. NOW is the time to do this. We start with the chattering French group, to send kindness and not inner barbs toward them when their endless talking takes over the spirit of the refugios. Then, with others, like the robust Austrian who seems so full of ego. He's walked the Camino before, plus many other trails in Spain. Seems to be doing it for sport only. Then there's the young Dutch woman in her twenties who bats her eyelids and flirts with male pilgrims, the reserved Englishman who says little and rarely enters into conversation, the Canadian who is warm and friendly one time, distant and aloof the next, and the South African gentleman who is always talkative but seems not to listen to others at all.*

> *Let them be. Let them have their own approach to life. Let them walk the Camino in their own way. The negativity that spews*

from my mind is simply that, a spewing of my own self, wanting others to match what I feel is best.

After all our conversations and experiences, one would think Tom and I surely learned the lesson about replacing negative thoughts with positive ones but this is a tough practice and we failed over and over. Each time we lapsed into negativity and failed to replace it with a positive we were led to see the flaw in our thoughts. In Villafranca a van and a car pulled up shortly after Tom and I registered at the refugio. A group walked in with spotless clothes, toting enormous suitcases. Next to our battered backpacks the suitcases looked like royalty. Most of the women wore make-up which was an anomaly on the Camino. This group was obviously a "walk-thru-the-camino-by-car" group. We pilgrims could see by their faces they were "shell shocked" at the refugio situation. The newcomers kept going up and down the stairs, whispering to one another and frowning. The rest of us pilgrims sat around on our bunk beds watching them and smirking at their distress.

After awhile the group came back up the stairs, grabbed their suitcases with a mixture of disgust and relief and returned them to the van. At the same time as they prepared to leave, Tom and I descended the stairs to walk into the business area of Villafranca in hopes of finding an internet café. Rain began falling as I stopped outside to ask directions from someone. When Tom and I turned to begin our walk, the driver of the van got out, walked over to us and asked ever so compassionately if she could give us a ride. Although we declined her kind offer, we knew, to our chagrin, another gesture of kindness had just come from someone we judged harshly.

The first time a pilgrim elicited a negative response from me that I couldn't replace with a positive was the night I stayed in Hontanas. A large, middle-aged Spaniard invaded our room with his three male companions. They talked loudly to one another and made boisterous comments about choosing one of the few open bunks. I grimaced inside as he clomped over to my side of the room to the open top bed across from my lower one. Sure enough, with a big thud, he threw his backpack down at the end of that bunk. Although it was not yet 10:00 p.m. when official silence was supposed to take effect in the dormitory, the overhead lights were out and many exhausted pilgrims were already sleeping.

The glow of the lights coming through the window and the open door created enough light for me to see a tall, heavy-set Spaniard with thinning, dark hair and a black, stubbly beard. I felt an instant dislike of him and found it difficult to extend a whispered greeting of hello. Part of me wanted to give him a lashing out about entering the room noisily and for not being more respectful of those already sleeping. Instead, I crawled into my sleeping bag with the thought he would surely be quiet soon. No such luck. He went on and on, guffawing loudly with his buddies. Finally, I rolled over and called out in Spanish, "SShhhh! Silencio en el refugio, por favor." He bellowed back, "It's not 10:00 p.m." He lunged up to the top bunk, swayed the mattress with his heavy body as he lay down, and continued his mouthy conversation in defiance of my parental statement.

I wanted to blame my angry irritability on my fatigue from the extreme heat of our seventeen-mile day but I was sure this was not the source of my emotional response. Something else caused my reaction. I rolled over and eventually went to sleep when he quieted down but before I did so, I lay there wondering how in the world I was going to return a positive for a negative with this pilgrim. Secretly I hoped not to meet up with him again on the route so I wouldn't have to deal with my judgments.

What a jolt I received when this same man appeared again the next night. This time I saw him in the early evening, consuming lots of wine at an outside table not far from the refugio. He came into the dormitory as loud and noisy as the previous night. As much as I tried to desist, I responded interiorly with even more negativity than before.

The situation challenged me to meet head-on my negative thoughts and unwanted feelings about him. I was puzzled. Other Spanish people were a joy for me to meet and greet. Why did I find this one hard to accept? How could I approach him positively? Was he meant to be a teacher for me? If so, what might his presence in my life be trying to tell me? I had not a clue.

In the meantime, I spoke to Tom about my struggle. Tom didn't have the same problem. In fact, Tom and the Spaniard enjoyed talking and laughing with each other. Tom even teasingly called the man "El Jefe" ("the boss") because he seemed to be the leader of his small group. El Jefe continued to cross our path time and again for the rest of the Camino, even on the last day as we made our way into Santiago. By then, I was able to replace my negativity with a somewhat more positive approach. How I thought he ought to act in the refugio was based on my own standard of behavior. My positive spin on this did not excuse what I thought was his lack of respect for pilgrims who were sleeping but it greatly reduced the energy I used to "fight him" in my thoughts and feelings.

One last thing about El Jefe: Before I left for Spain I read a story about a pilgrim on the Camino who yelled at another pilgrim for his loud snoring in the bunk bed above her. When I read that, I thought: "How awful for a pilgrim to talk to somebody like that on the Camino" but there I was, yelling at El Jefe for making noise. This, I think, is why he landed in my life. The Loving Guide of the Camino used this pilgrim to open another illusion of mine and toss it out the window.

RETURNING A POSITIVE for a negative is difficult to do and this lesson of the Camino continues to stretch me. When I find myself turning negatively toward another person, I recall those vivid lessons about not judging that Tom and I experienced on the Camino. Then I remember: every pilgrim is a story.

14
KEEP A STRONG NETWORK OF PRAYER

All the strength and love and faith in God
which one possesses, and which have grown
so miraculously in me of late, must be there
for everyone who chances to cross one's path
and who needs it.

—*Etty Hillesum*

Prayer motivates and sustains my life. This catalyst of transformation has evolved from various spiritual practices of mine through the years. No matter what the shape or form of my prayer, the core foundation of it remains constant. The basic focus is always communion with God and ongoing personal growth. This relationship not only continues to change me, it also unites me more profoundly with those who enter my life.

This understanding and orientation of prayer greatly influenced my time on the Camino. As Tom and I prepared for our journey, we both expected prayer to be central to what we undertook. While neither of us planned specifically for how this would happen, union with others through prayer became a central theme. This prayer wove through our pilgrimage in a wondrous way, creating a profound spiritual bond with others. As we moved forth on the Camino, prayer provided constant connection with those who believed in us and cheered us on our way. This bond generated determination and hope when we most needed it. No matter what joy or struggle we experienced, Tom and I knew love and courage were being extended to us through the prayers of others.

Prayer developed into its own shape and form on the Camino. During our retreat days in March, Tom and I created a pilgrim prayer which we planned to pray for the rest of our training and preparation, as well as each day of actually being on the Camino. We felt this prayer encompassed the hopes we envisioned for ourselves and for our world:

Guardian of my soul,
guide me on my way today.
Keep me safe from harm.
Deepen my relationship with you,
your Earth, and all your family.
Strengthen your love within me
that I may be a presence of your peace
in our world.   Amen

The first day after we composed the prayer we resumed our daily training walks. Tom turned to me that afternoon and suggested enthusiastically, "It's time to pray our new prayer!" With that, we began what would become a daily ritual on the Camino. Each time we walked, we started out side by side, joining our hand in the other's as we prayed the pilgrim prayer. Every day thereafter, whether alone or with each other, whether on the Camino or back home again, we included the pilgrim prayer.

We did not realize how this pilgrim prayer expanded our hearts. Saying those few lines deepened our awareness every time we prayed them. Each time the words seemed to draw us deeper into union with our Divine Pilgrim. Gradually, the prayer also bonded us with those we left behind at home. In due time, it brought us into fuller awareness of our oneness with other pilgrims. We shared this prayer with some of them. Eventually, it took us beyond that awareness and united us with all that exists.

Several situations presented themselves in which we chose to share our pilgrim prayer with others. First, Tom and I each wrote to our families and close friends, describing what our Camino journey entailed. In my letter I sent this promise:

I will take you walking with me as I venture out each morning. The first hour will be quiet and I will name you to God, one by one, as my feet are moving along (hopefully without blisters!) on the stony paths. I'll be taking you through small villages, up and down mountains, through large cities, down ravines, through fields, across the plains, and on into Santiago.

This correspondence included sending them our pilgrim prayer but we did it more as information than as an expectation for them to pray it with us. But they did pray it. Every day. Some posted it on their refrigerator doors or bathroom mirrors. Others used it to mark their daily prayer books. A few even set it on the middle of their kitchen table and prayed it before mealtime. Initially, however, this prayer was something we intended only for ourselves. We had not anticipated that everyone with whom we shared the prayer would want to pray it with us each day of our pilgrimage. How humbling and wonderful when we learned they decided to do this with us and for us.

The next surprise happened when Charlotte Huetteman, co-director of Emmaus House and Tom's spiritual director, offered to prepare a *sending forth* event for us. This gathering of prayer and friendship created a rich spiritual bond between us and the twenty or so people we invited to join us. Together we sang and prayed for a safe and enriching journey. After the prayer time Tom and I gave some details about the Camino, telling where we planned to walk and what the journey required. The two of us novice pilgrims even modeled our hiking boots, sunhats, and walking clothes for added effect. The group asked questions, offered advice, and laughed a lot as we all enjoyed Spanish "tapas" (appetizers). This event provided a delightful way to be sent forth.

After our return from the Camino, Charlotte again hosted a gathering with this same group. When we rejoiced and gave thanks in prayer and celebration, I suddenly realized that our Santiago pilgrimage began and ended at the Emmaus House. This retreat place is named after the beautiful Easter story in which the two disciples *walking on the road* with Jesus recognized him in the breaking of the bread (Lk 24:13-35). As I stood singing with the group, I, too, had a moment of recognition: "Ah," I thought, "like the disciples, Tom and I met the Christ as we walked the Camino in union with these friends and all we met on the road."

Another thread woven into this network of prayer occurred

through the phone calls and inspirational cards I received the month before leaving. One message in particular moved me deeply. A friend wrote: "I will be praying for you and Tom daily. It will be my way of making the walk with you. I will be praying for your feet in particular—and will image washing your feet at the end of each day. I often massage people's feet . . . it is a holy moment for me. So I will send comfort and healing to your feet." Notes like this assured me that what we needed for our walk to Santiago would be provided.

Once we actually walked on the Camino, numerous ways arose in which this strong network of prayer continued to develop. We received emails filled with encouragement and promises of continued prayer. These emails also informed us of people back home whose situations stirred our concern and care. Every day Tom and I named these people to God. Not a day went by without our connecting spiritually with those we left behind. It never felt like a burden nor did it distract us from the pilgrimage. Rather, it deepened our belief in the power of prayer and the possibility of being united in love even though we were many miles apart.

In the morning after we walked quietly for an hour or so, one of us would say to the other: "And who are we praying for today?" We then named these people as we walked, entrusting them to our Divine Companion. We also expanded our network of prayer to include the local people where we walked and the larger world, as well. When we prayed for people whom we did not know, we tended to pray for persons whose life or work somehow related to walking, such as those with disabilities who find walking painful or impossible, medical personnel and store employees who walk or stand for long hours, mothers of young children, etc.

One day we walked past a huge, open warehouse in which several men were loading stacks of large boxes into trucks. Tom and I moved past these men at the time the two of us were completing the part of our morning prayer where we remembered others. I looked over and thought of the tremendous amount of walking those workers did every day and added them to our prayer: "Those who stand all day in warehouses and factories." This aspect of our prayer kept our world from being too small and nurtured our sense of unity with people everywhere.

Tom and I were hesitant, at first, to share our pilgrim prayer with other pilgrims out of concern we might be pushing something unwanted onto them. One morning on the mesa, the two of us prepared to leave the refugio before dawn when Marie and Aileen asked if they could join us. These two pilgrims feared losing their way in the dark and thought if we walked together there was a better chance of their staying on the route. As the four of us left the refugio and stepped out onto the street, Tom and I looked at each other. We always prayed our pilgrim prayer out loud. We silently questioned each other with a look, "Should we pray it silently? Should we ask Marie and Aileen to join us?" Spontaneously, I called to the other two, "Do you want to join us for a little prayer we pray each day?" They looked surprised but responded positively so we told them about our prayer and shared it with them.

One source of prayer with and for others remained a mystery for awhile. Tom and I were not far into our pilgrimage before we started seeing small and large cairns (stacks of stones) along the way, usually by the side of the path but also on the top of fence posts, or in fields. Usually cairns are placed in out of the way locations as landmarks for direction but on the Camino almost every day we came across them, despite a well-marked trail. One day we found what looked like a little village of cairns, stacks and stacks of them next to one another, which pilgrims created along the path. We did not understand the full import of these until a Canadian mentioned to us that pilgrims place a stone on a cairn when they want to remember someone who needs prayer. From then on, when we passed a cairn we would pause, find a stone, and stand for a moment in silence remembering someone before adding another stone to the stack.

There were various creative ways of praying for others that

pilgrims developed on the Camino. One day we passed a large lumberyard that manufactured pulp. A huge linked fence ran alongside the place for at least a mile. Pilgrims passing by shaped small crosses from bits of discarded wood pieces and wove them into the fence links. There were hundreds of these small crosses on the fence. Another day we walked past crosses of stone that lay on the graveled path. It seemed everywhere we walked we received the message of staying united to others through prayer.

On September 28th we came to the most compelling prayer site on the Camino. We walked past the abandoned village of Foncebadón and came to the famous landmark, the Cruz de Ferro, located on the 4,900 ft. pass of Monte Irago. It was originally just a cairn marking the ancient path until someone Christianized it by placing a cross in the middle of the cairn. Guidebooks describe the cross as "one of the simplest, yet most ancient and symbolic monuments along the pilgrims' route." A cross of iron is attached to a sixteen-foot-long wooden stake rooted deeply in an enormous heap of stones. One pilgrim walking the pilgrimage for a second time told me the Cruz de Ferro had moved him more than anything else on the Camino. I understood why after I arrived there.

Traditionally, pilgrims for centuries have brought stones from their own home regions, carrying them a great distance to place at the foot of the cross in memory of someone in pain. Tom and I carried small stones from Iowa knowing we would leave them at the site. When we arrived at the location of the cross we made our way up four or five feet on the enormous pile of stones and placed our little ones among them. As we did so, I thought of all the crosses those varied-sized stones represented. I felt both humbled and inspired as I stood amid those stones around the cross.

As my hand let go of the two tiny stones I brought with me, I thought of how small the crosses of my life were compared to the huge burdens of others. I stood there and prayed for people back home who had tough crosses to bear. In this profound moment I united with these loved ones, as well as with all the other people in pain whom the rocks signified. With many other pilgrims who arrived there, we then sat down on the grass and reflected in silence for a long time. Finally, we rose to continue walking. The place had such a palpable sacredness to it. Part of me wanted to stay and absorb it more fully.

As we continued walking, however, my communion with those who suffer did not leave me. The strong thread of connection I felt at the Cruz de Ferro was not about to be severed. Not only did I continue to think about the prayerful scene of stones and cross, the scene also reinforced and rekindled my compassion during the rest of the Camino. To this day I can recall both my thoughts and emotions as I stood united with my own loved ones and with all whom those stones represented.

THE CAMINO OFFERED TOM and me an opportunity to experience more fully the strength and power of uniting with others in a spiritual manner. When the two of us returned home and sat once again in our circle of friends at Emmaus House, we shared with them some of the ways we had grown during our pilgrimage. As we did so, a deep resonance of gratitude filled me. I realized at that moment how much strength we gained because we united in daily prayer with our faithful relatives and friends. This network of prayer brought us home with a deepened appreciation of the value and power of joining our hearts with one another and with our God.

This life lesson is one I experience over and over in my life. Every day I sense the encouragement and sustenance I receive from those who promise to pray for me. Each day when I go for a walk the first thing I do is pray the pilgrim prayer. Then I consciously bring to God all those for whom I have promised to pray and those who have asked for my prayers. I intentionally unite each one with this God who knows the desires of my heart and who holds us close. The Camino reaffirmed my belief that this Great Love is an unbreakable link in our union with one another. No wonder the firm bond we have through prayer offers so much strength and support.

15
LOOK FOR UNANNOUNCED ANGELS

An elderly man appears and, despite our discomfort,
he chatters away in Spanish, while offering us some chestnuts.
He seems almost like an elemental wood spirit.

—Marilyn Melville

It seemed to take forever to walk out of Ponferrada. We left the refugio when traffic in the city of 50,000 peaked. We had a hard time finding our way through the busy streets. Most intersections were not marked with the usual Camino symbols of the scallop shell or the yellow arrow. Even when the streets were marked, the shells were usually pressed into sidewalk tiles instead of on the sides of buildings, making it difficult to detect the shells. To add to our frustration, it began to rain. As we moved along the street, we grew anxious because we had not seen a marker in quite some time. We looked up at the buildings, down on the sidewalk and all around for signs. To our relief, we spotted another shell imprinted on the sidewalk ahead of us.

We took about fifteen steps forward when I heard a rough voice behind me say, "This way." A blond-bearded man in a long, flowing, red rain cape motioned toward an alley to the right. On the wall of the alley, I noticed a yellow arrow pointing in that direction. Seeing it, I called to Tom but he missed seeing the arrow and hesitated following. I urged him to come. Then we both quickly turned and followed the silent pilgrim who was already moving rapidly down steep steps toward a park-like area along a wide river.

The tall man's cape blew in the windy rain and he reached out to wrap it closer around himself. He appeared mysterious, a bit sinister almost, as he hurried through the alley and down the steps with his head slightly bowed. I wondered about the wisdom of our decision to follow him on the route. Perhaps it was a ruse to lure pilgrims away for robbery. Several times others, like the French pilgrims, warned us to be wary of those who might want to rob us when we walked through larger cities like Ponferrada.

About the time fear flooded over me, I noticed he was taking us on an alternative path leading along a beautiful waterway lined with trees, a much more pleasant walk than through the busy industrial streets we left behind. His angular body and thin, long legs helped him move swiftly. We almost ran to keep up. We feared if we lost him, we might easily lose the direction of the path because there were few arrows on this route, as well. When we lagged far behind, he slowed his pace, and we were able to keep him in view. The red-caped man looked back once or twice to see if we were following. This pattern of his slowing down and our speeding up continued some forty minutes until we reached the edge of the city where it was obvious the central path lay ahead. Then the silent pilgrim picked up his pace and soon was nowhere to be seen.

Like the two on the road to Emmaus, Tom and I pondered that unusual event. How was it, we marveled as we walked along, that the stranger came by just at the moment of our need? How kind that he called out for us to follow him. What caused him to slow his pace so we could keep up with him? Why did he care enough about us to even bother to show us the alternative route? We both felt a certain mystical aura about the experience, almost as if the man was an angel sent to make our journey easier.

By mid-morning we finally found a place where we could stop for coffee. The rain continued so we took off our wet backpacks and left them outside the front entrance. We stepped inside and to our surprise we saw our "angel." We went over to him and thanked him for his kindness. One of us mentioned how grateful we were that he slowed his pace for us. At this he laughed uneasily and muttered, "Don't read more into this than it is." He followed this by saying it was only his mood that led him to walk slowly.

HIS COMMENT BROKE the mystical spell, but I still felt some divine intervention had blessed us. Although the tall man did not believe he was an instrument of God's goodness that day, we certainly did. This incident led me to think about how this sort of experience is actually more common than is supposed. People may not deliberately intend to be an instrument of God but they often are, without their realizing it.

The first time this happened on the journey we were en route to Spain. Because of weather conditions we arrived late into the Newark airport, causing us to miss our overnight flight to Madrid. It was 10:30 p.m. and we had not eaten dinner. We stood at the airline counter trying to understand the complicated directions for getting to our lodging for the night. The ticket agent looked exhausted and there was still a long line of passengers behind us to be reticketed. We jotted down the directions as quickly as possible so we wouldn't increase their waiting. Then we started down the concourse.

Neither of us had a clue as to where we were headed. A porter passed by us, noticed our confused looks, and asked if he could help us out. After a few moments of trying to explain, he said, "Here, follow me" and proceeded to walk with us for ten minutes to an elevator that took us in the right direction. As I turned around to say "thanks," he was already on his way, disappearing around the corner. In that moment, I had a strong sense we would be taken care of on the Camino. Even though I had fears and misgiving in the weeks ahead, I was quietly reassured that night because of this angel-like encounter.

While our red-caped angel appeared mysteriously and helped us out physically, another angel on the Camino surprised me by touching my heart. There were three times when I cried on the pilgrimage. The first time occurred when I experienced a hospitaler at the refugio in Tosantos. This refugio was one of the most welcoming places on the Camino. Much of this was due to his presence. He was a genuine hospitaler,[10] a robust Spaniard who laughed and smiled as he invited weary travelers in, often extending a warm hug with his greeting. His real name was José but Tom and I always referred to him as *Señor Cantante* (Mr. Singer) because he was full of music.

After most of us arrived in the late afternoon Señor Cantante invited pilgrims to join him in practicing songs for the evening prayer. We practiced several chants and the refrain to a great peregrino (pilgrim) song. His enthusiasm proved contagious. His brown eyes lit up as he introduced various melodies and affirmed our ability to sing the chants beautifully. As he directed us to soften the notes and keep the tempo, he sometimes closed his eyes in such a satisfying manner he looked like he was about to levitate. His sincere warmth easily permeated those of us present.

This enthusiasm extended into the dinner hour. Señor Cantante not only led the singing but he also helped to prepare and serve a massive pot of spaghetti with some carrots in it. An equally huge plastic mixing bowl of greens followed and then pieces of fresh fruit for dessert. He even passed a roll of toilet paper around the table when there were no napkins to be found! The conversation among the thirty or so of us that night rang out with both laughter and meaningful sharing. Much of it was due to the atmosphere Señor Cantante engendered.

After the meal we went up to the third floor where, of all surprises, we discovered a little prayer room off to the side with a tiny door through which we entered. I felt like Alice in Wonderland. The room had old round logs on the ceiling, a thin, tan rug on the floor, and cereal bowls holding semiwilted geranium blossoms in front of a faded hearth. We sat in a circle although there was barely room for all of us. Señor Cantante led us through the same prayer service as at the previous place, only we sang all the refrains plus the pilgrim song he taught us. I was thrilled to be singing, to have some music, because I had missed music so much. Even though my body was dead tired, my heart soared.

I am not sure exactly what this kind hospitaler triggered in my emotional response the next morning. We had been on the road for eleven days and maybe I just needed some attentive comfort and care. I only know that when we prepared to leave, Señor Cantante stood at the door to send us off. I thanked him for his hospitality and he responded by telling me it was a pleasure to do so for people like us. He then reached toward me, cupped my face gently in his hands, kissed me on either cheek, and blessed me with the farewell of "Buen Camino." An unmistakable touch of divine love filled that gesture. I sensed the power of a very special soul touching mine. Tears welled up and fell upon my cheeks. I looked to see that Tom was crying, too. My voice wavered as I bid Señor Cantante farewell in that poignant moment.

Other unannounced angels were on the Camino but none quite as significant for me as Señor Cantante. All the same, those we met blessed us on our way. Seventeen days after being at Tosantos, we encountered an unusual-looking angel in the guise of a village woman. It had been one of our days of persistent rain. She was obviously one of the elderly of the village and her face held an ancient gaze. The old crone had only one or two teeth in her mouth and dull-grey, straggly hair fell onto the side of her puckered, wrinkled face.

The elderly woman stood by her small house as we walked by in the rain. She waved us over to her with both hands, gave us a big, toothless smile and looked on us with concern, seeing how wet we were. This kind woman told us there was a place to stay nearby where we could find shelter and dryness. She seemed pleased to think she might be helping us. We considered the option, thanked her for her thoughtfulness, but decided to go on. It was too early to stop for the day's walk but her kindness served to remind us that we were cared for and protected. Her compassionate response provided us with some new energy of spirit as we returned to our walk in the pouring rain.

As I look back on our Camino days, many unannounced angels came into our lives at just the right time to help us with their considerate care: store clerks, refugio directors and volunteers, waiters and waitresses, farmers and city folk, and, of course, all those pilgrims who stepped forth when we needed them most. As I look back in reflection on what happened with our many "angels," I realize how fortunate we were to have someone there for us at the exact moment we needed them.

Since my return from the Camino, others have told me about strangers who offered them solace in a hospital emergency room, unknown people who stopped to help change a flat tire, unnamed persons who reached out to extend help or gave information at precisely the time of greatest need. These anonymous people rarely stayed for very long but their good deeds are tucked away in the hearts of those they assisted.

I have often wondered if people like the red-caped man, Señor Cantante, or the elderly woman knew how much their kindness mirrored divine benevolence. I doubt they did. I doubt that any of us are normally aware of having a profound effect on another unless someone tells us about it. We may do a good deed but unless the events are startling or unusual, they generally fade into life's experience without much of a second thought.

Yet, the slightest of actions may have a great influence on another. Each of us can be an *angel* in some way if we take the dictionary definition of *angel* as our source of description: *a messenger, a spirit or a spiritual being, employed by God to communicate with humankind.* And what do these angels communicate? For us on the Camino, they brought the message of God's compassion, kindness, thoughtfulness, and solace. We learned these angels are everywhere if the eyes of our souls are vigilant enough to notice.

The Camino helped me believe in the unique way God moves in our lives through the presence of other human beings who show up at the right time. Even when these strangers are oblivious to how they are an instrument of good, they act in a manner surprisingly beneficial and helpful. We never know when some-one we meet might be just the right person we need for the moment. We rarely expect unannounced angels in our midst but, oh, how wonderful they are when they show up to grace us with their gifts.

16

DEAL WITH DISAPPOINTMENTS

The secret of life, say the Utes,
is in the shadows and not in the open sun;
to see anything at all, you must look deeply
into the shadow of a living thing.

—Joan Halifax

No matter how well we plan our future, unforeseen disappointments are bound to push their way into our experience. There are always those situations that surprise us by upsetting our hopeful expectations and carefully planned agendas. We rarely make it through any journey without at least a few of these disturbances. They slip in no matter how vigilant we are. Disappointments can make our life either miserable or wiser. Sometimes both. So much depends on how we think about disappointments and what we do with them when they shove their way into our lives unannounced and unwanted.

The disappointments of the Camino showed up in myriad ways. Some of these were due to misconceptions and attitudes I developed prior to the pilgrimage. I must admit to having an idealistic notion of the Camino before I traversed it. I thought of it as a spiritual adventure where the spirit of welcome and goodness would naturally permeate the territory and all those who walked through it. My preconceived concepts also included a belief that the people of northern Spain would feel honored to have all these pilgrims tromp through their lands. My Pollyanna side assumed everyone would eagerly welcome us, that they would give us a respectful reception.

The first of my disappointments came quite early as we descended the Pyrenees. What a shock when some of the local people were distant and unresponsive to our greetings. When we encountered the townspeople, they were sometimes unapproachable, responding to our greetings with a grunt, a stern look, or no acknowledgment at all. How difficult it was to feel their cold stares and their apparent dislike of our walk through their land.

THIS BECAME MOST OBVIOUS to me on one of our earliest days when the Camino's route passed by a farmyard. The path narrowed and took us behind a barn. On one side was the wall of the barn and on the other side of the path were trees and a hillside. The local farmer had put a foot-high pile of manure directly on the path. There was nothing to do but trudge through this graphic and pungent message of annoyance. Being a farmer's daughter myself, I perceived why the owner had done this. My own father, who was quite a trickster, would have enjoyed seeing the "city slickers" tromping disdainfully through that pile of muck.

Those were the days when we walked through Basque country and, in spite of what I read about their history and how much they were challenged by invaders, I did not realize how fully their character was affected by their history of defense and protection. The Basques' effort to maintain their land, preserve their language, and continue their own way of life involved them in constant wars and repressive regional clashes from early years. "Perhaps," I thought, "this is the reason they are disgruntled and basically unfriendly."

As the days moved into weeks on the Camino, I understood more compassionately and clearly why the Basques responded coldly to us. It was not just their own history that molded their attitude toward those who walked the Camino. I discovered they had good reason for how they looked upon pilgrims. While other Spaniards along the Camino were much warmer and hospitable than the Basques, they sometimes also made it known that pilgrims were more of a nuisance than a blessing. When I observed how some pilgrims treated the earth and the local customs, it was easy to see why they would not be welcomed.

Pilgrims littered the land. I was shocked to discover this.

Everywhere Tom and I walked there was evidence of pilgrims' garbage. By the time I reached Santiago, I had seen thousands and thousands of discarded pilgrim items blowing in the fields, clinging to bushes, and filling the ditches. Plastic bags, yogurt containers, paper towels, toilet paper, soda cans, and plastic water bottles were everywhere. The invasiveness and carelessness of pilgrims appalled and saddened me. I couldn't believe people walking the sacred route to Santiago would deliberately desecrate and destroy it with their refuse.

On several occasions there were signs in fields posted by farmers asking pilgrims to please take their garbage with them. In a few refugios there were also notices asking pilgrims to be respectful and not trash the area. What made the pilgrims' garbage even more of a disappointment was that Tom and I noticed the efforts Spain was making to protect the environment. We saw lots of good terracing on farmland and evidence of considerable reforestation. Recycling was everywhere. Even in tiny villages, there were recycling bins, including bins for organic matter.

Some pilgrims irritate the local people because of their arrogance. They make no effort to speak Spanish yet they expect local merchants to understand them. At one restaurant pilgrims insulted a waiter by tossing a menu in his face and badly criticizing him because the restaurant did not serve what they wanted. Perhaps this is why (even though Tom spoke excellent Spanish) the owner of one bar where we went to buy a sandwich mocked our attempts to converse by responding in a very offensive way. He held up a toy cow, pushed it in our faces and made ugly sounds, laughing heartily all the while. It was obvious he had had it with pilgrims and the struggle with endless languages.

A few pilgrims embarrassed me by their deliberately obnoxious behavior. On September 7th as we walked from Pamplona to Puente la Reina, the route we walked was alongside a narrow two-lane highway. Three pilgrims walked past us on the road. As they continued on, one of them, a loud man with a large belly, deliberately stood right out in the lane of traffic and forced the driver coming toward us into the other lane. When the car swerved, the pilgrim laughed about his ability to cause the driver to veer off to the side.

These disappointments were good "wake-up" calls to me, reminders to watch my own actions and see where my attitudes and expectations also caused offense. I realized that even if I were cautious, I could still infringe upon the customs of others without being aware of it. I became more conscious of this when we stopped for lunch at Hornillos. We bought some cans of juice at a bar and sat outside on a bench in front to eat our bread and cheese. As I took the first bite of bread, a woman stepped out of a door next to our bench. She started yelling loudly at us in an angry and agitated voice. Tom and I both jumped up and I asked, "Is this your bench?" and we apologized profusely. This was not the problem because she continued to gesticulate wildly toward us and then toward the street, becoming more and more vehement.

We continued to think she was upset with something we had done but finally understood it was not about us. It was about some pilgrims who stopped before us and tossed their dry, leftover bread into the street. Perhaps they thought birds or animals would eat it but it was a tactless deed. Had these pilgrims been observant, they would have seen that people in the villages keep their streets meticulously clean, sweeping and washing them every day. Tom and I felt badly about this situation. We again apologized to the woman and went into the street where we picked up what bread remnants we could. The woman calmed down and began speaking in a more friendly tone to us but the damage was done. Once more, pilgrims were seen as an annoyance and, once more, I was disappointed with how we pilgrims alienated others by our carelessness.

Much of the time pilgrims simply did not think of how their actions would affect the people whose lands they traversed. There were pilgrims who boasted of their taking apples from trees or clusters of grapes from vineyards. The pilgrims didn't realize that if hundreds who passed by daily each took an apple or a cluster of grapes, the fields would soon be empty. The same was true of those who took shortcuts off the trail. Vegetation was quickly damaged by pilgrims trying to save a few minutes of time and energy.

I NEVER GOT USED TO the fact that pilgrims were a composite of humanity with diverse personalities. It took me several weeks before I could swallow my glowing ideas of a perfect Camino where everyone respected and cared for others and the land. The disappointments of the Camino forced me to accept that people who walk as pilgrims are the same as people everywhere else. Each pilgrim has strengths and weaknesses and everyone brings these with them on the pilgrimage, just as we all bring ours on the road of life. Because of this reality, nothing is in perfect harmony for very long. Whenever I was disappointed, I had to take a long, painful look at my unreal expectations of whatever it was that disappointed me, including my own inner responses.

This was certainly true for my most surprising disappointment. We reached the last segment of the Camino with only a day or two before we walked into Santiago. Only a short distance separated us from the cathedral of St. James, the destination of our pilgrimage. How astonished I was to find my feelings not being at all like I planned for them to be. My expectation was that I'd be absolutely thrilled to reach the outskirts of the city. I presumed I would feel pure elation because I finally arrived at the end of the journey but heartfelt joy eluded me.

I did feel relief at the thought of not having to stay in another refugio or deal with food problems. A sense of satisfaction visited me when I thought of walking over 450 miles, arriving safely and in relatively good health. What jolted me was that I mainly felt an immense sadness, not joy. I couldn't believe my hollow feeling.

One pervasive thought kept circling my mind: "The Camino has ended." The long anticipated pilgrimage, the endless days of walking, everything I experienced, all this was coming to a close. The thought of not walking anymore, of not having beauty, adventure, and discovery in the heartbeat of each day, of not meeting new pilgrims and facing daily challenges, all of this caught my heart and overwhelmed it with melancholy and emptiness.

The sadness was hard to shake until some latent wisdom rose to the surface in me. As I faced my feelings and disappointment, the Buddhist teaching about not clinging to what one has and enjoys came to mind. "Ah," I said to myself, "I need to appreciate the gift and hold it with gratitude, being willing to let go when the time comes." As I walked into the city of Santiago, I recognized that the sadness of endings which I felt was another call to let go, to hold my journey with gratitude and trust. The future would unfold and all would, indeed, be well.

Soon after Tom and I arrived at Santiago, an Australian pilgrim expressed one of her disappointments. Rachel was a remarkable woman who walked the Camino alone after her friend fell and broke her leg. She seemed both wise and courageous. I valued her insights so I listened carefully as she told me how she was moved to tears of joy and thanksgiving when she arrived at the cathedral. She was greatly put off, however, when she walked into the church to give the traditional hug to the statue of St. James and saw the donation box next to it.

Rachel was also disappointed with the Mass the next day, the culminating event of the pilgrimage. She thought Jesus, not St. James, ought to be the center of attention and that his statue, not St. James, should be above the altar. Rachel also felt the *botofumerio*, the enormous incensor that takes eight strong men to swing it up toward the cathedral's ceiling, was a circus spectacle and not at all appealing. Her disappointment further intensified when she saw how people pushed one another in the crowded church in an effort to receive communion.

As I listened to Rachel speak of her dissatisfaction regarding the liturgy, my own Camino disappointments revealed themselves for what they were: mainly a result of my own ideas, values, and expectations. It became clear to me that no one set out to deliberately cause me undue discontent. I was the main cause of the frustrations I experienced. This insight helped me to understand Rachel's disappointment. She unsuccessfully hoped the liturgy would meet her theological and spiritual expectations. The pilgrim Mass in the cathedral was rooted in a strong medieval history that did not suit her style or type of prayer. Rachel was disappointed because she expected something different.

Once again, the Camino taught me a vital lesson. I looked at the disappointments Tom and I experienced, including the smaller ones, and saw how they were largely due to what we imagined or hoped would be. For instance, we read in the guidebook that Arca was in a beautiful eucalyptus forest. So all day we talked about and imagined this wonderful place. We could imaginatively smell the eucalyptus long before we got there but when we actually arrived in Arca it was not at all what we had anticipated. It was anything but exquisitely beautiful in our eyes.

The same was true with other expectations. Communal prayer in the refugios, or rather the lack of it, disappointed us. We wrongly presumed each refugio would offer evening prayer for the pilgrims but this rarely happened. We were also surprised and dismayed when one of our pilgrim friends had her walking sticks stolen in a refugio. We thought all pilgrims could be trusted. We longed for vibrant Eucharistic liturgies but, with a few exceptions, most of the parish Masses were dull and unappealing.

Even some of the historical aspects of the Camino disappointed us. How disheartened we were in Logroño where we looked at the front of a church door and saw an engraving of St. James Matamoros depicting his killing of the Moors. As we stood looking at the art, Tom turned to me and commented: "Jesus would be amazed and appalled to see that on the door of a church."

The disappointments I experienced on the Camino led me to ask numerous questions: "Is it wrong to have ideals, goals, and hopes for what might be? Is it disastrous to have expectations and longings? Is it unreal to think that life's situations might match my own values? Is it crazy to believe that things might turn out as one wishes?" My response to these is: not at all. But when something does not match my desires, I have a choice. I can crab about the situation or see it in the light of unmet expectations. Attention to expectations can keep me from blaming and carrying anger around unnecessarily.

My CAMINO DISAPPOINTMENTS also taught me a better approach to life. If I expect every day to be harmonious and trouble free, I will be disheartened and discouraged. If I think I can plan and arrange my day so well that nothing will enter in except what I want to have there, I will be frustrated and full of irritation. When I recognize disappointments and accept them for what they are—experiences where my expectations are not met—then I can approach them in a much calmer and more growthful manner. Disappointments along the way of life do not need to sidetrack me from a life of joy and gratitude.

17
SAVOR SOLITUDE

There is no true solitude,
except interior solitude.

      —Thomas Merton

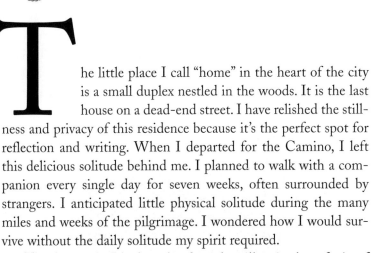

he little place I call "home" in the heart of the city is a small duplex nestled in the woods. It is the last house on a dead-end street. I have relished the stillness and privacy of this residence because it's the perfect spot for reflection and writing. When I departed for the Camino, I left this delicious solitude behind me. I planned to walk with a companion every single day for seven weeks, often surrounded by strangers. I anticipated little physical solitude during the many miles and weeks of the pilgrimage. I wondered how I would survive without the daily solitude my spirit required.

The first night I laid my head on the pillow in the refugio of Roncesvalles I felt uncomfortable in the crowd of unfamiliar persons. Not one single, tiny space gave me room to hide out and be by myself. I felt sure I'd never meet solitude again until I was back home. I was mistaken. Solitude was there, only not in the way I normally found it.

During the first week on the Camino I discovered solitude rather easily once I was willing to accept it in a new shape and form. Instead of being all alone in a physical space without other people around me, I found interior solitude by going inside and spending time there. All I had to do was deliberately turn within and dwell in my inner space.

A daily pattern developed which helped me find this solitude. Tom and I would arrive at a refugio, register, unpack, wash clothes, take showers, and then settle in for what was often at least

a three-hour wait before the evening meal. Tom was content to lie
on his back in his bunk, journaling and mapping out the next day's
route. The first place I found for solitude was also my bunk bed.
With strangers less than three feet from me, the rustle of backpacks being emptied and filled, conversations of weary pilgrims in
the background, I quickly learned how to pull an invisible cloak
around myself for brief periods of time.

What a joy to sink into the solitude of this psychological and
spiritual space. I turned inward to the solitude I yearned, never
disconnecting physically from the world around me but closing
the door in that direction. I purposely separated my inner world
from the outer one to commune with the deeper part of my self.
This interior solitude supplied a great solace and a source of
encouragement. It gave me daily strength to meet the physical
and emotional ups and downs of the Camino.

No matter where the place or space, I discovered I could be
alone by putting on my invisible cloak of solitude. When staying
on my bunk bed got tiring, I sought quiet places outside. I sat on
stone steps and benches, straddled an old stone wall, enjoyed
shaded grass under trees in local parks, placed myself on sidewalks
and leaned against the outside walls of refugios. Some places
especially lent themselves to reflection, like the lovely town park
in Cizur Menor with its aspen, poplar, and short beech trees.
These trees were friendly, hospitable receptionists, welcoming and
giving me room to tend my overcrowded psyche. Being in that
space allowed me to empty out the many thoughts and feelings
crowding my inner landscape.

Other places of solitude were uncomfortable like the small
back yard behind a bar which offered housing upstairs. I don't
know what was worse, the wobbly white plastic chair that kept
tipping sideways or the strong smell of cabbage plants nearby. In
the laundry area behind the Arzúa refugio, I wedged myself into
a corner and sat for an hour on a very low stone ledge in front of
a weathered blue door. In spite of my cramped legs, I found the

way into interior solitude and managed to relax somewhat.

Even with pilgrims bustling around me I could find solitude. I felt peaceful and at home with myself in the Grañón refugio when I wrote in my journal:

> *This refugio has a nice spirit. We are so fortunate to have found it. Thanks to Tom. The 100 bed one at Santo Domingo would not have been like this. I look forward to all of us gathering later for "cena" (dinner) tonight. Right now I sit at a table. Across are two Frenchmen plotting the next day's walk. In the corner, a young woman strums a guitar. People keep going up and down the creaky stairs to the right. Another man plays cards alone at the end of the table. A young woman and man read books from the small library—a few shelves—against the wall. (No books in English.) I do so love this pilgrim scene. It is easy for me to be alone with my inner world in the midst of these fellow travelers.*

The solitude I sought on the Camino gave me thinking time to review and take note of how life events and people affected my thoughts, attitudes, and emotional responses. Solitude allowed room for relating more intently and intimately with the divine. Time with myself cleared out the cobwebs of worry and concern, restored my balance when I was grouchy and irritable. Going into my interior space helped maintain my sanity and regain my composure when the difficulties of the walk threatened to steal my joy. In this space I leaned back and recomposed myself.

This interior solitude, along with the steady rhythm of walking mile after mile, served as a catalyst for deeper awareness. The solitude I found and savored on the Camino had an amazing effect on me. The busyness of my life slowly settled down as the miles went on. For a good portion of my life I had longed for a fuller experience of contemplation, that peaceful prayer of the heart in which one is able to look intently and see each piece of life as sacred. Ten days into the journey, totally unforeseen, the grace of seeing the world with startling lucidity came to me.

My eyes took in everything with wonder. The experience was like looking through the lens of an inner camera—my heart was the photographer. Colors and shapes took on nuances and depths never before noticed. Each piece of beauty appeared to be framed: weeds along roadsides, hillsides of harvested fields with yellow and green stripes, layers of mountains with lines of thick mist stretching across their middle section, clumps of ripe grapes on healthy green vines, red berries on bushes, roses, and vegetable gardens. Everything revealed itself as something marvelous to behold. Each was a work of art. I noticed more and more details of light and shadow, lines and edges, shapes, softness, and texture. I easily observed missed details on the path before me—skinny worms, worn pebbles, tiny flowers of various colors and shapes, black beetles, snails, and fat, grey slugs. I became aware of the texture of everything under my feet—stones, slate, gravel, cement, dirt, sand, grass. I responded with wonder and amazement. Like the poet, Tagore, I felt that everything "harsh and dissonant in my life" was melting into "one sweet harmony."[11]

On September 15th I wrote in my journal:

Today I realized it has taken me many days of walking to finally reach a clearness inside that is allowing me to contemplate all I see. It was gradual—beginning with the magnificent grapes in the vineyards. Now I can look at this old bench I sit on, rusted green, bird poop, highway noise nearby, and I can be still inside. I can look at the shape of the bench, the holes, the patches of corrosion and "see" it with my "special eyes." I need to "see" people's faces more, to read the sacredness there, too.

Interior solitude cleared a space in me for contemplation. The rhythm of my body gradually balanced the rhythm of my spirit. Walking steadily in a relaxed manner without pushing and rushing allowed me to behold life instead of simply hurrying past it. Going slower was essential for this contemplation. The further I walked, the more my senses became alert and alive. Being close to the earth added to this awareness. Tom remarked one day, "We can sure see a lot more walking than we ever could in a car." He said that about the time I spotted a chubby black mouse scurry across our path.

That same day we walked to the abandoned *ermita* (hermitage) shown on our Camino map. It was a large building with a beautiful wooden entrance and splendid tile on the veranda. We sat in front of the *ermita* on a stone bench while we ate our lunch. I sliced a tomato with my Dad's old pocket knife and thought of him as we put the tomato slices on our bread with cheese. Tom and I shared one carrot that I scraped and an apple cut in half. While we ate, we marveled at a colony of ants scurrying away with our bread crumbs. When we got up to continue our walk, the beauty and simplicity of our lunchtime struck me as I mused out loud to Tom: "When was the last time we ever watched ants?"

This sort of contemplative moment reawakened communion with the divine. While I did not participate in much formal or structured prayer on the Camino, prayer enveloped my whole day. Because of inner solitude and the steady rhythm of walking, the entire day gradually became a spiritual moment where union with God was inherent in everything. Prayer became a contemplative oneness with all creation.

Waiting was another catalyst for interior solitude and contemplation. I doubt I ever waited as much as I did on the Camino. Maybe it just seemed that way because I had nothing else to do but walk. Once the day's journey was complete, that was it, except for washing clothes and eating. I waited to get into refugios and then waited to get my pilgrim passport signed. I waited for the next little town to appear on the horizon when I thought my legs would go no further. I waited in line to wash clothes, to take a shower, to use the toilet. I often waited for several hours for restaurants to open in the evening. I waited for night and longed-for rest.

In OCebreiro, we arrived by noon and decided to stop for the day. The rest of the afternoon I waited for the heavy fog and rain to lift so we could explore the historic village and find a place to eat. As I waited, I sat and pondered the past five weeks' journey, wondering how the Camino was shaping me. After awhile, I opened my little book of Tagore's poetry and read: "*. . . I know not how I am to pass these long, rainy hours.*" In the next poem I found this: "*I will fill my heart with thy silence and endure it.*"[12] God was surely encouraging me to savor solitude.

At home a multitude of things vied for my attention. On the Camino, few things distracted me. I had one thin, little poetry book to read, no music to enjoy, no correspondence, nothing. Doing nothing can be difficult when you're used to zooming along through the day, never getting everything accomplished that you hoped you would.

Waiting drew me inward and plunked me down in solitude. Having nothing to do led to greater interiority. In León when I was recuperating from illness, I lay all day on my bed, grateful to be quiet, to be inactive and resting. I spent a good portion of an afternoon in that room watching fat pigeons on the roof across from my window.

I noted this before I went to bed in O Cebreiro:

> *To do nothing, to be, to wait on the weather, to wait to "go to bed," to wait "to eat," to wait to go to the tienda (store) . . . I have sat, laid down, rested, prayed, read, and reflected on Tagore, journaled, watched the rain-fogged window, listened to the steady raindrops—basically, I am at peace. But I long to be active, to do, to walk around, to see the sights . . . and all I can do is wait here out of the rain, grateful for the dryness, for the warmth . . .*

Although I still grew restless when I had long hours of "doing nothing" on the Camino, it taught me much about solitude and gifted me with countless opportunities for contemplation. When first on the Camino, I thirsted for books, magazines, and newspapers. But after contemplation took hold of me, I gradually let go of needing to fill my mind with so much "stuff." In fact, when I returned home and started reading again, I felt I was cramming too much inside my head and actually chose to do little reading for several weeks. I didn't want to lose the ease with which I was able to unite with life around and inside of me.

One other highly significant part of the Camino led me into solitude and contemplation: walking the extensive miles of high plains of the mesa. It takes at least a week to walk this long flat stretch. Some pilgrims skip walking this section because of intense heat, lack of trees for shade, and the absence of mountains. Some describe it as "a boring landscape." For me, the mesa was an essential part of my growth on the way to Santiago. Perhaps more than any other part of the ancient route, this section pulled me inward and emptied me.

The mesa has its own "is-ness" that sustains and holds one on the path. It does not contain the usual enticement of outer landscape (the mesa does have its own beauty) but it offers the beauty of solitude and silence. It is a tough place to walk: long, grueling days in the hot sun without anyplace for shade, endless sameness of fields and roads. Even coming across a little hill becomes "an event" on the mesa. These journal entries hold descriptions of it:

> *Tom and I did well today on the mesa. It is so different from the rest of the Camino. All our energy is into walking and drinking enough water. Bearing the sun. Almost no shade. Until now, the walk was energizing with the beauty we saw. Now, the landscape is mostly the same. Emptied fields of grain. No mountains. No clouds in the sky. Some big piles of stones in the fields. A cluster of trees (2–3) every few miles. Clumps of bushes now and then. Brown-toned landscape. Yes, all this will draw us inward. I wonder if all the mesa is this way? What else will it do to us, for us?*

We did not see this town of Hontanas until we were literally almost on top of it. We walked flat, flat, flat land and then came to this small valley. There it was, hidden away. So different from our past weeks where we saw the pueblos in the distance before we arrived. (SEPT 19)

Tall grasses by the road, harvested wheat fields, plateaus in the distance. That's all. Except for a tall, steep, mile climb up to a flat area early on today. I can see how one turns inward here. There's little diversity exteriorly. The road is all the same except for a few curves. No trees. Few animals. I do continue to see and marvel at the wildflowers, little yellow ones, blue ones, and one bright yellow sunflower. How did it survive in all this heat and dryness? (SEPT 20)

The walk seemed to never end today. On and on. Tom remarked how little we spoke, and that it was okay with him. I agreed. The mesa is an extrovert's nightmare of loneliness and an introvert's dream of solitude. It seemed to me that the mesa could be that way, anyhow. Tom and I have both grown quiet. Many tiny gifts of beauty: flowers, butterflies, small green bushes, old stones, etc. (SEPT 23)

We both wanted to walk the complete mesa but several days later I became extremely ill and soon after Tom was also whipped by sickness. The mesa conquered us. After we recovered, I jokingly remarked, "The flat mesa flattened us." This was more true than I cared to admit. Some weeks earlier, a Belgian pilgrim who had walked the mesa before, told me with a Mona Lisa smile to look for surprises on the mesa. He said it was a grand opportunity to grow. I now understood what he meant.

ON THE MESA insignificant things of life sink into oblivion. The self is forced to let go of what is unimportant as the journey itself takes the pilgrim along. All else is forgotten as one plods along—

mile after flat, hot mile—enveloped in the silent solitude that provides growth. The miles and miles of walking evoke the emptying of self so that life is seen with renewed clarity and all that one values is put into its proper place.

Eventually I understood what Eckhart Tolle wrote in *Practicing the Power of Now:*

> *Presence is needed to become aware of beauty, the majesty, the sacredness of nature . . . To become aware of such things, the mind needs to be still. You have to put down for a moment your personal baggage of problems, of past and future, as well as all your knowledge; otherwise, you will see but not see, hear but not hear. Your total presence is required.*

Our mind gets skewed with illusion and our heart tilts toward emotional imbalance without time alone. As life gets progressively frenetic and our days increase with activity, the times and places for solitude are fewer. They get squeezed into the tiny leftovers of the day. Yet, our spirit cries out for some seclusion, for distance from what threatens to crush the life out of us. The temptation is to ignore this plea for what will change and recharge us.

SOLITUDE IS POSSIBLE, even for the busiest and most pressured of people. The key is to be intentional about finding a bit of space and time in the day. This might be in the shower, car, or subway, before a computer, or at a cash register. Ingenuity and creativity are required to find solitude but the first step is to believe in its worth and to desire it. Since my time on the Camino I have found solitude in many places, including waiting in long lines at airports, standing at the supermarket checkout, and vigiling by the hospital bedside of a loved one. (My old invisible cloak of solitude comes in handy.)

The Camino swept me up into the wondrous arms of inner terrain and gave me eyes to see my outer terrain in a new way. I discovered I can find solitude and prayer anywhere and anytime.

All I need to do is be intentional about claiming this space. Inside of my solitude. I recover perspective and enter into communion with the Holy. Solitude may not include physical aloneness but I can always find interior space to reflect on life and commune with the One I love.

18
HAVE A SENSE OF HUMOR

We both found it a relief to laugh,
and we shared our amusement at something
neither of us could fully comprehend.
—*Peter A. Campbell & Edwin M. McMahon*

The Camino is not for the faint of heart. It is a tough road to walk. Despite the beauty, adventure, mystery, and joy it contains there is also the challenge of putting one foot in front of the other mile after mile. Pilgrims are often exhausted at day's end, nursing blisters, strained muscles, or sprains from falls on the road, miserably wet from unending rain, or sick from bad water, colds, and flu. Without laughter as a daily companion Tom and I would have had many more irritable times, cranky attitudes, and discouraging days. We learned to laugh at how crazy we often looked, at the mistakes we made that cost us time and physical energy, at the unappealing condition of some of the refugios, and at the hilarious stories other pilgrims shared with us.

We learned on the Camino the value of taking delight, seeing the incongruous in situations, enjoying the humor of others, and not taking ourselves too seriously, particularly when things were not all we wanted them to be. This lesson started during our preparation time before we ever began the pilgrimage. When we first wore our heavy hiking boots and carried our backpacks on the local trails, I was embarrassed. Iowa is not an area where people need to use frame backpacks when they hike. I thought we'd look pretty foolish. I certainly *felt* silly wearing mine.

Some bikers and walkers did stare and laugh at the two of us trudging along with our heavy packs in the intense summer heat and humidity. Surprisingly, though, most people on the trails cheered us on. They often called out various comments to us: "Looks like you're in training. Going to the mountains? Good luck. Good for you! Where are you going? Hope you have fun." What was initially embarrassing gradually held an element of pleasure because of their comments.

One day a man in his seventies, and another guy who looked like his son, biked past us going in the other direction. Tom and I hiked a few more miles, reached the seven-mile marker and then turned around to walk back to the starting point. These guys on the bikes also turned around someplace and were now headed in our direction again. As they zoomed past and saw us heading back, the older guy yelled, "So you didn't find anyone at home?" It's amazing how a funny comment like that instantly helped to cheer our hearts.

Later that day, a plump woman with lots of white hair flying out around her helmet also passed by, a box of cookies neatly tucked in a carrier behind the bike seat. That gave us both a good chuckle. She had a great smile for us as she called out, "I tell myself I'm having fun! Hope you are, too." That little message enlivened us because we were thoroughly worn out by then.

A week or so after that, on a steamy August day, Tom and I met early before the sun was too strong so we could walk several hours. Many bikers and quite a few walkers were also on the path. As a couple was walking past us, the man jokingly asked: "Are you two running away from home?" These funny comments were the sort of thing that kept our spirits high. The enthusiasm and joy of others reminded us of the adventure awaiting us.

I DON'T THINK either of us realized how soon we'd need humor to keep us enthused when we were actually on the Camino. It was just our second night when we faced the option of laughing at the craziness or letting ourselves get bogged down in it. The refugio where we stayed in Zubiri was terrible. This old schoolhouse was one of the worst of the entire Camino. Inside it there were eleven sets of bunk beds all scrunched together in the room, placed so close to one another we barely had room to put our packs between them.

Among the twenty-two of us in this room were men and women from many countries. The only place to dress and undress was on one's bed. The south side of the room consisted of all windows without shades in which city lights shone through all night. There was one toilet for all the women, including another room full of pilgrims, and four soiled showers without any doors or curtains. The bathroom was so small the door would barely close without first sitting down on the toilet. Foul air filled the room because of the number of people and the windows being unopened.

Tom and I were in top bunk beds, next to each other. He put his little flashlight on so he could map out the next day's route. In attaching the light to his bald head like a coal miner's lamp he accidentally snapped his head with the band that held it in place. The custom of silence began in the refugio at 10:00 p.m., so we tried to stifle our snickers. Later, Tom had trouble getting into his sleeping bag and we started giggling again. Once he got into the sleeping bag he looked so funny, unshaven for two days, earplugs in, and his black blindfold on his forehead ready to pull over his eyes. I made a face indicating how weird he looked. He leaned over and whispered: "Oh, if our friends and family could see us now!" This line became one of our mantras when things got bad and it never failed to help reignite our enthusiasm for the pilgrimage.

Another refugio that required a sense of humor was in Estella. There, too, the toilets and shower situation challenged us. Here both men and women used the two toilets and the one shower room. The next morning it was comical. I stood in the bathroom next to a tall Frenchman brushing my teeth at the only sink there. We had to take turns cleaning our toothbrushes under the faucet. We both starting laughing. As he and I left, a woman came in to brush her teeth. Just as she got to the sink, she dropped her toothbrush on the floor. I thought she'd faint at the sight of it on that filthy floor. We both exclaimed "arrrrgh!" at the same time. (I didn't hang around to see if she actually used her toothbrush after that!)

It helps to laugh at oneself, too. Humor in this case takes the edge off of what might otherwise be tough to accept. Tom and I both walked slower than most other pilgrims. It was not easy to have them constantly pass us by. One day Tom got the idea of giving us each a nickname. We called ourselves *La Tortuga and El Caracol*, the turtle and the snail. When pilgrims greeted us as they hurried by we often called out our nicknames to them. They laughed and we did, too. Giving ourselves these nicknames helped us accept our slowness and affirmed our desire to walk in a relaxed manner. Our joking about it gave us the freedom to not worry. Like the turtle and the snail, we arrived at where we needed to be eventually, just not as soon as the others. It was surprising how much ease developed by using these humorous nicknames.

On the way to Tosantos, laughing at myself also alleviated my embarrassment and revulsion. This situation occurred on our twelfth day and by then I had gotten used to the fact that there were no public restrooms on the Camino. The local bars in the villages always provided a place to stop but oftentimes we walked many miles with no villages in sight and on occasion the only bar in town was closed. This meant finding a tree, a good-sized bush or even a large rock to squat down behind to relieve myself. All the pilgrims were in the same predicament and we learned quickly how to find a hidden spot along the path to take care of our full bladders.

This particular day when I really had to *go*, there was no village, no tree, no bush, no stone, and far too many cars and pilgrims passing by on the road for me to find a place. Finally I spotted a little row of trees about 100 yards off the road. They were tall, thin trees so I knew I'd have to be quick about it. Well, I was so quick that I peed in my left sock and boot. I was aghast and angry but by the time I got back to the road I was laughing. It wasn't long before I'd forgotten how irritated I'd felt. (I did give my socks an extra good washing that evening.)

Laughing at ourselves even included the emails we sent home. Four days of no sun and our sneezy, runny colds led us to look for ways to remain positive about the current situation. As we sat by the computer in Triacastela, Tom wrote to his friends, "I can't hold it in any longer. The truth is, we are not on the Camino in Spain. We are on the beach in the Bahamas and have been sending you our imaginative descriptions of the Camino. Know that you have not wasted your prayers. We have been passing them on to the true pilgrims and also applying them to ourselves, so we don't get too sunburned on the beach. Thanks for supporting us." Just thinking about getting a sunburn when we walked in all that rain left us chuckling on our way back to the refugio.

By October 1st we were quite adept at allowing our sense of humor to keep us balanced in wretched situations. Thank goodness, because this day we got caught in an enormous downpour. It was about 1:00 p.m. and we were two miles from Ruitelán and the next refugio. We walked all morning along the Valcárcel river in a steady drizzle. When the rain started coming down in sheets we stood under a thickly leafed chestnut tree but it offered little protection so we kept on walking, barely able to see. That afternoon's rainfall was the one in which pilgrims who got caught in it talked about for days. For the first time on the Camino Tom and I got completely drenched. Our socks and the inside of our boots squished with water. Our rain jackets and tee shirts were totally soaked. The rain even permeated our waterproof backpacks, which were covered with garbage bags. By the time we knocked on the refugio door in Ruitelán we were a sorry, dripping sight.

We didn't start laughing then. We were too miserable. After two hours, five other pilgrims arrived just as sopping wet as we were. The tiny room of four bunk beds consisted of cramped quarters in a space only slightly larger than my bedroom at home. The mattress on our bunk bed was the only personal space we had. About then we started to experience things that made us chuckle. The first of these was after the sun reappeared and we went outside to hang our wet stuff on the clotheslines.

The clotheslines hung over a treacherous, rocky mound slick from the rain. It was dangerous to climb and we had to be careful not to break our necks when we stretched upward to hang the clothes. One couldn't help laughing at how ridiculous it was. Because there wasn't enough room on the lines, the French couple across from me hung some of their wet things on the edge of the open space of their bunk bed. At one point Pierre crawled down from his mattress and parted the wet clothes to peer in at Michele to see how she was doing. Those two started to giggle and soon all of us in the room were giggling, realizing how funny it was for Michele to be hidden behind their damp clothes.

It was a long afternoon. We had to wait until 7:30 (over six hours) for dinner. It started raining again, which meant we were confined to our tiny room. I napped, journaled, prayed, and read some Tagore poetry (my only book). Then I got bored so I decided to number all the pages in my journal. I was oblivious to everyone's hearing the swish of the turning papers. Tom finally called up to me from the bottom bunk, "Hey, what in the world are you doing up there?" When I told him, he hooted loudly and that caused the rest of the pilgrims to join in the laughter. Such simple things humored us, but it was vital that we let ourselves be freed from stress by opening up to these little amusements. Otherwise we would have been consumed with misery in that confined space, which smelled of wet woolen socks, soggy clothing, and strange body odors.

Two nights before Ruitelán, we stayed in a new refugio in Ponferrada with small rooms and only two bunk beds in each room. One of the pilgrims we shared the room with was a Canadian woman in her early twenties. She was in the top bunk above me and her body odor and clothes smelled like neither had been washed in weeks. That night after I went to sleep, she hung her red sweater and towel down on the top edge of my bunk. When I got up in the middle of the night to go to the bathroom, my face hit the sweater. The stench was horrific. I said to myself, "You know, God, you have a miserable sense of humor." I then managed a wan smile and went on my way to the bathroom, able to find a bit of humor even in that smelly moment.

Laughter came to us often and easily on the Camino. The night we were in the lovely town of Villafranca, situated on the Burbia river, we met Antonia, an older Dutch woman. She was delightful as well as knowledgeable about the Celtic history of the area and full of stories as she imbibed from her large container of rosé wine. As we shared our impressions of the Camino, we told Antonia we were surprised to see so little wildlife in northern Spain. Antonia responded that her idea of "wild life" was the refugio where people arose and left at 5:00 in the morning to begin walking. She then told us of a night when she heard a pilgrim get up and rustle around in his backpack. She thought it was morning so she got up quietly and dressed in the dark. It was only then she looked at her watch and noticed it was 2:45 a.m. So she flopped back down on the bed, hiking boots and all, and went back to sleep.

THE GIFT OF HUMOR lifted us out of our discouragement and tiredness countless times. The Camino taught me how the irony and incongruity of a situation can ease the pain of it. Having a sense of humor doesn't take the toughness of the experience away but it softens the distress, changes the focus a bit, and allows one's spirit to recoup some of the lost energy. We never used laughter on the Camino to criticize others or to put ourselves or anyone else down. That approach would have been a destructive way to use humor. Humor was a friend to us and for us. Laughter left us feeling more at peace and ready to let go of what did not turn out the way we planned.

Having a sense of humor saved us from many a tough day. It

unleashed stress and brought a return of enthusiasm so we were not smothered by our own dashed hopes and expectations. Humor enlarged our view and helped us to see that a new day followed, that we didn't have to be right all the time, that our mistakes could be forgotten and our hope regained. This lesson is a valuable one for all who take themselves too seriously or who live from day to day in a situation that threatens to overwhelm them. Three cheers for a sense of humor.

19

TRUST IN THE DIVINE COMPANION

What would it be like to open our hearts to fear,
to befriend it with wonder,
as one would a deer in the forest?
—*Dawna Markova*

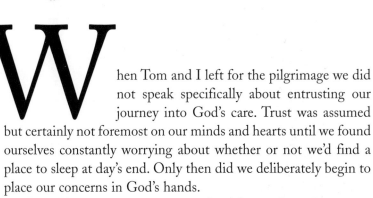

W hen Tom and I left for the pilgrimage we did not speak specifically about entrusting our journey into God's care. Trust was assumed but certainly not foremost on our minds and hearts until we found ourselves constantly worrying about whether or not we'd find a place to sleep at day's end. Only then did we deliberately begin to place our concerns in God's hands.

It strikes me as quite amazing, how fear and worry creep in without our even realizing it. Equally surprising is how faith-filled people so easily overlook the basic requirement of the Camino: to give oneself over to God's continual presence and guidance. Why is it that Tom and I waited until the going got tough before we started leaning on the One who promises to take care of us? With the risk taking, the unknowns and uncertainties, coupled with the considerable dangers and struggles the Camino holds, certainly trust in God needed to be primary for us.

Amazingly, trust did not boldly enter the picture until we found ourselves caught in anxiety on the Camino. In late March during our retreat in preparation for the Camino, I suggested we write down and then talk about our fears and concerns. My list seemed rather lengthy when I shared it with Tom:

• Blisters on my feet and weakness of the left leg will make it difficult to walk or I will develop other physical difficulties.

• I might become irritable, become a problem for Tom and me walking together.

• I'll get separated from Tom on the route, lose him, not find him again until Santiago.

• Something will happen to him, like falling and being hurt.

• One of us will get very ill.

• We won't be quiet enough to truly look at and enjoy the beauty of the landscape.

• I will feel inadequate and "out of it" because I can't understand the language well enough.

• It will be boring when we are not walking. Nothing to do (no reading, music, computer).

• I won't be able to eat in a healthy way.

• Someone I love will die while I am away from home.

I made lists like this in the past when facing something risky and unknown. It didn't matter that few of those fears ever became a reality. Even though I learned to lean on God in times of travail and trouble, new uncertainties and worries stirred inside me, challenging my peace of mind and heart as I prepared for the Camino. Talking about them with Tom helped ease my apprehension. Tom had fewer concerns and fears. He provided a lot of good assurance that things would go well. Tom was always the more optimistic and hopeful of the two of us.

To offset our concerns, we created positive statements (affirmations) in which we named our hopes for the Camino. Both of us wanted to believe all would be well for us no matter what happened along the way. We decided to say these affirmations every morning on the Camino. These positive statements served as a reminder to approach our pilgrimage with a spirit of confidence:

1. The Camino is a wonderful adventure for us.
2. Our physical, emotional, and mental health is excellent.
3. We have no blisters. Our calluses are not a problem.
4. We find beauty everywhere.
5. Our relationship with God, each other, and self grows and deepens.

6. We enjoy speaking Spanish with those we meet. We gain
   fluency.

As I look back, I recognize that trust in God, while not
specifically named in those affirmations, was certainly implied.
Still, we had to talk about this issue of trust explicitly soon after
we began our trek to Santiago because of our daily circumstances
and anxious spirits.

On just the second day of walking the Camino, the word
"trust" entered my journal vocabulary:

> *I am trying to be open, to be present, to live in the NOW. I think
> I am slowly doing so. Today I believed we should trust that we
> would find a place to stay. Heard there was a fiesta in the town
> toward which we were walking and there would be no room.
> But, no problem. I must trust about food. About everything! Yes!*

Two days later, after Tom and I left Cizur Menor and walked
toward Puente la Reina, we discussed how we were feeling. We
both wanted to walk in a relaxed manner and acknowledged we
fretted and worried way too much, trying to walk far enough and
fast enough to ensure finding a place to stay in a refugio. Neither
of us wanted to feed this anxiety all the way to Santiago. Then
Tom remembered the Spanish phrase: *Primero Dios* (God first).
What the phrase suggests is that if one puts God first in life, then
all will be well, no matter what happens. It implies trust and confidence in God's abiding providence. We decided to use the
phrase whenever we heard one or the other of us becoming apprehensive about anything.

We found that phrase on our lips often during the next six
weeks. *Primero Dios* gifted Tom and me with a conviction that we
would be taken care of and each day we would find a place to stay.
We still forgot from time to time to rely on our Divine
Companion. This was especially true the first time we encountered the harvest fiestas. We read about the September celebrations taking place in the small towns but what we did not realize

was that privately run refugios closed to allow the owners and staff to join in the fiestas. The celebrations also meant that hostels and inns had fewer vacancies due to tourists and other visitors. Yet, these fiestas provided an opportunity for a growing confidence as we searched to find housing.

In each fiesta town, we managed to secure a place. Sometimes it was a private refugio not listed in the guidebook, or a hostel, an inn, or even a restaurant with rooms above it. The saying is true that God helps those who help themselves, but it is equally true that God guides us to what we need. When housing seemed impossible to find, Tom always came upon someone who had information about a place with rooms for rent or a refugio not on the map.

In Azofra, the public refugio was full due to the fiesta but the director told us we could sleep on the kitchen floor. The only space on the cluttered, greasy floor was right by the front door, directly in the path of oncoming pilgrims so we decided to seek alternate housing. I waited in the kitchen while Tom went and sat in front of a private refugio a block away, in response to a sign on the front door saying the owner would be back shortly. Tom waited for two hours before someone told him the refugio was closed for the season. He then searched the village and found several rooms still available at a local inn.

This sort of thing happened again and again. Ten days into the journey I wrote:

Primero Dios is good for us—we have been taken care of. Each day we are never sure . . . today we were to stay on the third floor, a cramped room with mats crowded in next to each other on the floor. Tom asked about the toilets at night as he would have to go all the way down to the first floor where the men's toilet is. The hospitaler listened to Tom very compassionately and then showed us to a closet-sized room. It is on the side of the building right next to one of the busiest highways I've ever heard. Semi trucks galore zoom along, several every other minute, and they do not slow down for this small village. In our "private room" there are two horrible cots with soft, ugly mattresses. Nothing else. But we are so pleased to be off the crowded floor and for Tom to be closer to the restrooms.

Food, the ongoing challenge, also required that we trust. We carried some provisions with us but not very much because they weighed heavily in our packs. Several times food was not available in the villages where we stayed. Fortunately, we almost always kept some supplies in our packs to provide a meager meal. On those occasions we ate what we had in the hope we would find some place open for breakfast along the road the next day. We usually did, but a few days we walked many miles before we ate.

As our walk brought us near to the mesa, I reflected one night:

> *I am sort of anxious to get walking the mesa and sort of dreading it. It's the great heat and dryness that concerns me. I hope we can do it. I also grow concerned about food and housing. It is time to trust again. The heart of the pilgrim journey is to trust God's providence. Primero Dios!*

Our most challenging experience in regard to food took place on October 6th after we consumed most of our food for lunch. The day before we checked our guidebook and it noted two bars that served food in Eirexe, a village of about 100 people. Sure enough, upon walking into the village around mid-afternoon we spotted each of the bars. Neither was open but we were not concerned—it was siesta time. Later we returned to check the times for evening meals, only to discover one bar was closed for the season and the other would not be open because the owner was at a funeral. By then, it was too late to walk to the next town for food.

Between the two of us we had one small tin of tuna and a handful of almonds. Nothing more. Things didn't look too good for having an evening meal. Once again it was time to trust. *"Primero Dios,"* we said to each other as my stomach began to growl.

Tom spoke with Maria Paz, the refugio director, who first led us to the refugio's tiny kitchen. We looked in the cupboards with hope that previous pilgrims left something behind. No luck. Maria then suggested we go next door to a woman who often sold food to pilgrims in similar situations.

We went to the neatly painted house and knocked and knocked on the front door. Finally a woman answered. We obviously disturbed her because she looked at us with a determined scowl. When we asked if we could buy some bread, the unreceptive woman muttered "no" vehemently and shooed us away with a look of disgust as she slammed the door.

With that rebuff we went back to the refugio where Tom rested and I sat out front to write in my journal. I told myself going without food was not a problem, it could be a good experience to fast from food. Many people in the world were without food at that moment. Going without food offered me a chance to unite with them in spirit. But I had walked many miles that day with little food and I felt weak. I knew that even if I didn't have any nourishment that night, I'd have to walk a ways the next day before we found a place with food. As much as I tried to convince myself I didn't need food, my body kept telling me something different.

Things looked a bit dismal for us and the other twelve or so pilgrims who also arrived with little or no food in their packs. Toward evening when we were sure we would all go without a meal, Maria told Tom she arranged for a local man, Oscar, to take us in his car to a *supermercado* (supermarket) in another town. *Primero Dios!* We quickly gathered the other hungry pilgrims and together we made a basic grocery list: pasta, onions, tomato paste and red peppers for making sauce, lettuce and tomatoes for salad, bread, and red wine.

At 6:00 p.m. off Tom and I went with Oscar, zooming along to the supermercado. We went back on some of the same roads we walked that day. (We commented how quickly the miles sped by in the car!) Oscar went in the store with us and helped us find the best red wine. Then he left to pick up his daughter from school, telling us he was coming back soon. The two of us hurried through the store to find our grocery items as we did not want to delay Oscar. We stood outside for about ten minutes with our plastic bags of groceries when he pulled up, his preteen daughter in the front seat with him.

Tom and I attempted to put ourselves and the food in the back seat. A lot of stuff was stacked high inside the small car, so I squished in next to Tom as best I could, bags of groceries piled on us and around us. But just then, Oscar went off to "do some business." He said he would be back shortly but we waited and waited. The thirty minutes or so we sat there seemed like hours to me.

While I struggled to remain peaceful, Tom, in his usual caring way, spoke with the daughter who was initially ill at ease with us. They had a wonderful conversation about school and other topics while I stewed about getting back. I knew the pilgrims at the refugio expected us much sooner and we still needed to prepare the meal. Finally Oscar returned, drove us back and dropped us off at the refugio at 7:45 p.m. When Tom held out money to pay for gas, Oscar refused to take it. He gave us a big smile and said, "Give it to the saint" (St. James). *Primero Dios!*

All the pilgrims helped to prepare the simple meal. What a challenge to do so in a kitchen with almost no utensils and dinnerware. We found an odd assortment of items: mostly tablespoons with which to eat our spaghetti, bowls and pan lids for plates, plastic glasses and odd-sized jelly glasses for wine. A large, beat-up tin tub held the lettuce and tomato salad without dressing. Everything tasted absolutely delicious and we ate voraciously. Amid much laughter and entertaining conversation, we discovered it was Yvonne's birthday. We toasted her with what remained of our two superb and very inexpensive bottles of wine. It was my happiest meal on the Camino.

THE EXPERIENCE OF THAT evening meal taught me a lot about believing in God's care especially when external conditions point to the opposite. I became aware of how quickly my trust falters when things do not go as I hope. I too easily become discouraged when things do not go my way. To trust means relinquishing some of my strong need to have control when I face uncertainty and insecurity. My own strong efforts do not completely guarantee I will have inner serenity and peacefulness.

That surprising and wonderful meal at Eirexe also taught me that one ought never give up hope. Maintaining confidence is of utmost importance, no matter what the situation. The Camino reinforced a major lesson of life: the heart of the pilgrim journey is not about being anxious and fretful. It is about putting God first and trusting in this abiding presence and providence. With this faith-filled assurance, the peace of the Camino readily takes up residence in every pilgrim's heart.

20

LET YOURSELF BE HUMBLED
BY WEAKNESS

O fool, to try to carry thyself upon thy own shoulders!
O beggar, to come to beg at thy own door!
Leave all thy burdens on his hands who can bear all,
And never look behind in regret.

—Rabindranath Tagore

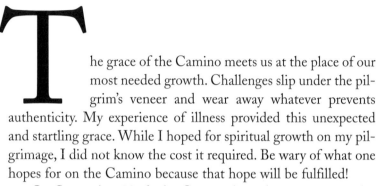

The grace of the Camino meets us at the place of our most needed growth. Challenges slip under the pilgrim's veneer and wear away whatever prevents authenticity. My experience of illness provided this unexpected and startling grace. While I hoped for spiritual growth on my pilgrimage, I did not know the cost it required. Be wary of what one hopes for on the Camino because that hope will be fulfilled!

On September 22nd, the Camino brought my strong independent nature to its knees. After almost three weeks of walking, I felt strong in body and spirit, confident I could handle just about anything that came along. My self-sufficiency was soon caught off guard. We headed toward Ledigos, a hard day's walk on the mesa. A hot wind blew in our faces most of the eighteen and a half miles, making the walk more difficult. Tom and I were both famished so we stopped about 2:00 p.m. at a bar in Calzadilla de la Cueza to eat. I ordered a Spanish omelet with ham. We talked a bit with several other pilgrims who had also stopped, snitched a few of their delicious green olives, and then left to walk the remaining four miles to Ledigos.

About twenty minutes beyond Calzadilla de la Cueza, my stomach rumbled and churned. As this discomfort continued, I turned to Tom with concern, "I feel really weird. My stomach has a squirrel running around in it." Not long after, my feet and legs would hardly move. I walked bent over and held my stomach, intent on keeping my body going. Tom urged me to stop. "No," my strong self said to him, "I think I'll be okay." I wasn't okay. I was terribly nauseated, even weaker, and ready to faint. After five minutes more of dragging myself along, I gave up. Tom helped me off the trail where I slipped out of my backpack and collapsed in a ditch of tall, dusty weeds.

The strong, sturdy woman who strode out into the freshness of the morning lay in the dirt and prickly brush, trying to vomit. I feared not being able to get back up again. Tom told me later how concerned he was while he sat with me, seeing my face dripping with perspiration and drained of color. Several times he asked, "Do you want me to go to the road and flag down a car? We can take you to a hospital." His suggestion was totally unacceptable. I couldn't bear the thought of anyone having to take care of me or of my being a burden to Tom. Worst of all, I didn't want to stop my walk on the Camino. "No, no," I insisted, "just let me lie here for awhile. I know I can do it."

After staying in my collapsed position for about a half hour, I raised myself up with Tom's help. Though I was weak and unsettled, I felt determined to go on to the next refugio. Because Tom was unable to carry two large backpacks he helped me as I struggled to put mine on. By then, we had three miles to go, uphill most of the way. I felt frail as I walked hunched over, moving ever so slowly. A car stopped on the highway a short distance to our right. I looked over and saw a group of tourists get out of the car and take our picture. I was photographed in my worst moment and must have looked pathetic. I was too sick to laugh but days later I remarked, "That moment was certainly a lesson in humility. Instead of moving along in my best pilgrim's stride, there I was, barely able to maneuver."

My lesson in humility was only beginning. All I could think of on that last stretch was how much I wanted to be horizontal, not vertical. "Oh, if I could just lie down," I kept repeating to Tom. When we finally arrived in Ledigos, Tom explained my physical condition to the woman in charge. I didn't even stop at the desk.

After practically crawling up the flight of stairs, I dropped onto a mattress on the floor. The rest of that day and night is a blur but I remember how lovingly others ministered to me.

An older woman knelt down and helped me drink a soothing cup of special hot tea "for nausea." Another covered me with a blanket. A pilgrim who was a nurse checked me for fever. As I lay there, pilgrims came and went around me, asking how I was doing. I heard myself mumble weakly that I felt very ill. I not only felt physically miserable, I felt vulnerable and dependent, a state not often experienced in my "regular" life. A voice inside urged me to receive from others, to let go of my need to handle things on my own, to accept others' help. It was time to listen to that voice.

I could do little else that night except be with my sick condition. Whether the illness was caused by food poisoning, bad water or something else remains a mystery. I do know I stayed awake in great physical discomfort most of the night. There were seven other pilgrims in my room. Tom was on the mattress next to mine. Across from him another man and woman slept. To add to my misery, as the night wore on the man across from Tom snored. This snoring was the worst I heard on the Camino. Although I was exhausted, his noise kept me from going to sleep.

Eventually, I arose and walked over to where the man slept. I poked him on the leg with my foot in hope that he would awaken and stop snoring long enough for me to fall asleep. My movement failed and his snoring grew even louder. From across the room I heard a female voice with an English accent whisper, "Kick him again, harder!" As sick as I felt, I grinned in the dark thinking, "So much for the pilgrim spirit!"

Sleep was impossible for me that night. The next morning I felt incredibly washed out and still nauseous. While other pilgrims setting out appeared fresh and ready to go, I felt fragile and weak. Noticing my plight, a friendly Brazilian youth gave me a handful of the same herbal teabags that temporarily soothed my stomach the night before. After most pilgrims left, Tom and I talked about what to do. We were unable to stay in the refugio because it closed by 8:00 a.m. If we walked slowly, I thought I could make it to the next place. I drank only sips of water during the ten miles of that long day. Without Tom's kind and considerate presence I could not have managed. He continually offered assurance and compassion.

The only place along the entire Camino with benches every mile or so happened to be on that day's segment. How fortunate to have those places for rest. I willed myself to get from one bench to another for long breaks. Each stop was humbling. I wanted to be strong. No matter how I tried, I could not make myself strong. I was unable to walk any faster. In spite of how much I desired to feel better, I could not force myself to do so.

At the end of the day we stayed at a hostel where I fell into bed in the late afternoon without eating all day. I slept until we left to walk again the next morning. While I remained nauseated, a tiny bit of energy returned, enough to help me walk another twelve miles. Along the way, a German woman suggested I drink Coke to help settle my stomach. This home remedy offered some relief. That night another German couple, who were also ill, shared some homeopathic pills for nausea. These pills along with the anti-nausea medication Tom purchased at a pharmacy helped greatly to ease my discomfort.

By the third day, I snacked on little bits of bread. In the late afternoon we found a private refugio at El Burgo Ranero where a lovely white-haired lady greeted us at the door. We unpacked and went to buy provisions for the next day. While we were in the store, Tom turned to me and said, "I don't think I can stand up. Can you help me back to the refugio?" I looked at him in alarm wondering if this was the same illness as mine or something else, like a heart attack. As carefully and quickly as we could, the two of us went back to the refugio with Tom leaning on my arm. The solicitous owner of the refugio knocked on Tom's door several times in the early evening to see if he was all right. Tom's illness included diarrhea and the next day we learned many pilgrims had the same thing. Most blamed it on contaminated water.

I knew I had to try to eat something besides bread. Because Tom was sick in bed, I went alone at 8:30 p.m. to the only eatery in town to hopefully find something bland for dinner. I longed for chicken soup but knew there was no chance of it being on the menu. I explained my situation to the waitress and wondered if I could have plain pasta instead of the pilgrim's meal. The waitress looked doubtful but went to check. Out came the cook who yelled "No" from across the room when I again asked for "pasta solamente." She would make no exceptions and told me I had to eat el menu del dia.

Having no choice, and no other place to go, I received the regular fare. The first course was a large *ensalada mixta:* tomatoes, red peppers, green olives, and a big stem of canned asparagus on a bed of lettuce. Normally, I was thrilled to have vegetables. This night I ate about three pieces. When the main course of fried potatoes and pork came, I sat looking at a full plate, knowing my stomach could not tolerate it. After about five bites in fifteen minutes, I left the rest of the food and went back to the refugio.

Because diarrhea still plagued Tom the next morning we decided to take the bus to León where we could find accommodations and wait until both of us felt well enough to be back on the Camino. This was a huge decision because we both wanted to walk the entire route to Santiago. I read about pilgrims who skirted some of the harder parts of the Camino, taking taxis or buses part of the way. Taking the bus seemed like "cheating" to me even when pilgrims did so for health reasons. Now we were in a similar situation. Tom could not walk because of his diarrhea and I needed to recoup my strength. If we stayed in the little town instead of riding the bus to the city and recovering there we would lose several days of walking and perhaps not make it to Santiago in the days allotted. The city also had more medical help if we needed it. Once again, the Camino exposed my pride and challenged my independent nature.

How humbled I felt as we rode on that bus to León. Far off to our right pilgrim after pilgrim, with their heavy packs weighing them down, walked on a tree-lined path. As I watched them walking, I knew how it was to be one of them. I imagined the tiredness of their bodies and wondered which ones had sore feet. I felt united with them, knowing how much time and energy it took to walk from one refugio to the next. A sense of betrayal nagged at me because of my taking a bus ride equaling two days of walking.

The dashed hope of being able to walk every step to Santiago pressed in on me. Taking the bus meant I would not walk all 500 miles of the route because I was too weak to manage it. I was not as strong and independent as I thought. Riding the bus to León was one of the hardest things I did on the Camino. After we settled into a hotel, I wrote in my journal:

> *What is this all about? I don't know. Can only stay open to the moment and hope for the future—that we will regain our strength and be able to go forward with healthy bodies. The mesa has "flattened me," stripped me, not just of securities and nice things, comforts of home. It has forced me to rely on strangers, to be at the mercy and goodness of hostelers, of pilgrims, of the elements. I do know that here I am "just a pilgrim," my persona is of little value; it counts as naught. Only that I am a woman, a human being, who is walking this ancient path, for some unknown reason . . .*

> *A big letting go for me. I thought I'd walk every single kilometer of the Camino and never take a bus. But it felt right to be on the bus today, to save my energy. Yet, when we looked from the bus and saw fellow pilgrims weighted down with their packs, bent and walking the road we would have been on, I felt a deep kinship with them. And I wished I was there with them. I realized*

*in that space of time on the bus that I have become a pilgrim! I
am one of them!! It took the objective distance of being in the bus,
looking out at them from my weakness, to fully realize it. I
thought, "I want to be there with you . . . I would prefer it to
being on this bus ride. I will be there again with you on the way."*

Strange as it may sound, while I longed to be a pilgrim when
I was riding the bus to León, the next day as I rested and regained
my energy in the hotel, being a pilgrim lacked appeal. My sickness knocked both physical and psychic energy out of me. A
morose mood full of discouragement set in. I was shocked to feel
antipathy toward every difficult thing I experienced on the
Camino. I did not want to admit the Camino had gotten beneath
the veneer of my self-determination.

Several days after being in León, I named and acknowledged
my emotional process:

*During these days of illness, I have hated being in Spain and
have longed for home. I've despised all the pilgrim things one has
to accept, especially the smells: walking regularly through sheep
and cow manure, mustiness of the rooms at night, bathroom
sourness, dust of boots, the raunchy odor of my own clothes, even
though I wash them out daily.*

*I've hated the food, particularly the dry white bread. I've hated
the pattern of walk, walk, walk and hoping to find a place to
sleep at night. I've hated carrying my backpack and caring for
my feet.*

*I've not had energy to talk much with Tom. Could only survive
by putting all my energy into "one foot before the next"—now,
finally, today, I feel that gradually I will be able to come alive
again, to be more energetic, hopeful, positive. I've said little about
how I despised all the pilgrim things, how I wanted to get off the
road and go home. Never have I really thought to actually do so
but the feelings were there. Today I want to go forward. I want*

to be a pilgrim again. Why am I doing this difficult thing? I do not know . . .

Slowly I learned and accepted the lesson of not trying to be in charge of how I walked the Camino. Gradually I accepted that the Camino was walking me. As Tom's diarrhea lessened the second day at León, I had a disappointing reoccurrence of nausea and weakness. But this time I readily agreed when Tom suggested we again take the bus, this time to Astorga for one more day's rest. As it turned out, this extra day was just what both our bodies needed. We left a day later from Astorga sensing some renewed strength, grateful our bodies were in condition to walk again. How good it felt to be back on the road, walking toward the beauty awaiting us in Galicia.

From that time onward, sporadic stomachaches occurred until I arrived back in the States. I also caught a nasty cold, which most of the pilgrims developed in the cool, damp area of Galicia, but I did not rail against my physical limitations again. Those minor ailments were simply the Camino's way of reminding me who was in charge of the journey. I no longer took my strength and good health for granted, no longer believed I was invincible, no longer needed to go the road alone.

THE CAMINO STRIPPED ME of my ultra-independence and readied me for future situations to meet this kind of challenge—perhaps in illness, in failure and difficulty or unexpected chaos, and most certainly in the aging process. None of us can continually live without the help of others. No matter how independent our American culture encourages us to be, life situations arise in which we need to humbly and gratefully allow others to do that which we cannot do for ourselves.

The Camino convinced me that I cannot "carry myself on my own shoulders." Life moments will require me to receive from others. I must allow them to help me with my burdens. Next time my heart will be more open and ready to accept a helping hand.

21

ENJOY EXISTENTIAL FRIENDSHIPS

We are pilgrims on the earth and strangers;
we have come afar and we are going far.
—*Edward Sellner*

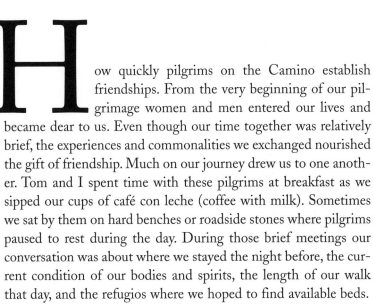

How quickly pilgrims on the Camino establish friendships. From the very beginning of our pilgrimage women and men entered our lives and became dear to us. Even though our time together was relatively brief, the experiences and commonalities we exchanged nourished the gift of friendship. Much on our journey drew us to one another. Tom and I spent time with these pilgrims at breakfast as we sipped our cups of café con leche (coffee with milk). Sometimes we sat by them on hard benches or roadside stones where pilgrims paused to rest during the day. During those brief meetings our conversation was about where we stayed the night before, the current condition of our bodies and spirits, the length of our walk that day, and the refugios where we hoped to find available beds.

In the later afternoons we often met these same pilgrims when we completed our day. We chatted with them as we washed our clothes by hand or waited in line to take a shower. We often sat together at an evening meal, caught up in animated conversation. We joked with them in bathrooms that were pitifully small and dirty, and we pained with one another when one of us became injured or ill. Yet, pilgrims rarely shared email or postal addresses. It seemed an unspoken agreement that the friendship of pilgrims stayed contained within the space and length of the Camino.

Not every pilgrim we met became a friend. A number of folks were simply acquaintances or mutual pilgrims on the way. With some, the language barrier prevented us from getting to know one another. With others we shared only a fleeting greeting or a brief conversation. Even when we engaged in longer conversations with some pilgrims, these did not always develop into a special bond of understanding and care. We counted as friends the pilgrims with whom we felt a resonance of mind and heart.

Among these friends were pilgrims whose lives kept weaving in and out of ours as the Camino took us westward. We gravitated toward one another as our paths continued to cross. Our mutual enjoyment and appreciation of each other grew with each connection. About the time we thought we would never meet up with someone again, they appeared at some café, bar, or refugio. It was always a joy to see a friend we lost track of due to walking at diverse speeds and staying at different places. When we met pilgrims we had not seen for awhile, a hoot of surprise filled the air. Hellos were called out and hugs of welcome followed as we greeted pilgrims we thought we had lost but who suddenly materialized.

Sometimes these friendships grew slowly. The first time I met James the Englishman he said little and seemed to be uninterested in conversation. One night we sat across from one another at a table in the refugio. James appeared withdrawn. Noticing he was always alone, I hesitantly inquired, "What made you decide to walk the Camino?" He looked at me, sizing me up before he spoke. Then he replied softly, "I decided to walk it with my daughter and her two college friends. They walk a lot faster than I do. They're up ahead somewhere. We'll meet in Santiago."

With this snippet of conversation James entrusted me with some personal information. This gave me an insight into his situation. From then on, our paths met numerous times. Each time, James was a bit more talkative. Eventually, I even teased him about his "English reserve." We lost track of James for awhile but after another week, he was at the same refugio as ours. An amazing thing happened when we saw each other. James, who initially came across as distant and disinterested, actually gave me a hug.

FRIENDSHIPS ON THE CAMINO often developed in a domino fashion. I recall the time I refound a pilgrim who took some days off to rest her sore feet. Patti eventually used the bus to make up for those days of rest, coming into Santo Domingo on the same afternoon Tom and I walked into the city. When we saw one another in the plaza Patti called out, "Joyce and Tom! Where have you been?" She proceeded to embrace the two of us like we'd known each other for years, rather than a few days. Then she did something that was often the source of a new friendship on the Camino. Patti turned and introduced us to Liam, a middle-aged man from Northern Ireland whom she just met and who began the Camino that very day. We then befriended Liam who, in turn, introduced us later to Sean, his Irish friend and walking partner. This is how fresh friendships often formed. One pilgrim met another, who met another, and another.

We knew pilgrims by first names only. It was enough. The first pilgrims we met were a couple named Tony and Joan. What made this initial meeting especially significant is that they were also Americans and the first pilgrims with whom we conversed at length. (We did not know it at the time but we would meet very few pilgrims from the United States as we walked the Camino.) Tony and Joan were coming out of the inn at Roncesvalles as Tom and I looked for the marker to start our walk on the Camino.

"Do you know where to find the entrance onto the Camino?" Tom inquired of them. "No," Tony replied. "We intended to start looking for it ourselves. Where are you from?" And that's how our friendship began. We easily connected with these two because of some immediate, common characteristics. Like us, Tony and Joan spoke English, were Roman Catholic, and about our age. Their friendliness and openness appealed to us. All four of us eagerly asked questions of each other as we stood by the La Posada Inn, sharing our thoughts and feelings about the first day's walk soon to begin.

Although we never planned it, the four of us often stayed at the same refugios during the next two weeks. A special camaraderie developed. Tony and Joan told us they were only walking three weeks. They planned to take a bus from Burgos to Astorga in order to have enough time to complete their pilgrimage to Santiago. I pushed away the fact they would not be around in two weeks. I liked them too much to think I'd never connect with them again. When it came time to bid farewell to Tony and Joan I felt sadness and regret, knowing I would never see them again. They brought much joy into my life in a short amount of time.

Another set of American pilgrims whom we met early on were Patti and Elaine from Wisconsin. Elaine planned to walk the entire route but Patti intended to walk only halfway due to commitments back home. One memorable time when our paths reunited was on the seventh day when Tom and I took an afternoon off. We walked more miles than planned in our previous days and decided to take a break.

We found a great refugio run by Dutch Reformed volunteers in Villamayor de Monjardín, which is situated among rolling hills of cornfields and splendid vineyards. As we walked up to the refugio, there sat Tony and Joan. We were elated because we did not know they planned to stop there. No sooner did the four of us, plus about a dozen other pilgrims, get our packs to our bunk beds and settle in when we heard more familiar voices. Up the steps to the dormitory came Patti and Elaine. My heart leapt with the prospect of two more pilgrim-friends spending the evening there.

ELAINE GREETED US with a big hello and then complained, "Can you believe that thick mud we trudged through all morning?" Her question led to our own grouses about the tough walk up steep hills. Then all six of us picked up our messy boots and went out to a water trough to wash the heavy red clay off. We laughed as we scrubbed the stubborn clay and groaned about how hard the trek had been. From there we each went to do our daily hand-washed laundry. We hung our wash on the terraced roof's clothesline so the warm sun could dry it.

On the terrace we discovered some old chairs where I plopped down to enjoy the beautiful view. Elaine soon joined me, letting the sun dry her freshly washed hair. On another corner of the roof, Tom went and sat down next to Patti and Joan. I don't know what they spoke about but Elaine was a member of the Sierra Club so the two of us launched into some mutual endeavors of ecology and the need for well-monitored environmental programs. From there we spoke about Barbara Kingsolver's books and soon connected in kinship through other authors we mutually read and enjoyed. These kinds of situations fed our Camino friendships.

Later the six of us joined a Japanese couple sitting in the warm sun by some small tables in front of the refugio. We sat there sipping beer and wine, enjoying the easy, relaxing time. Suddenly the energy cranked up a few notches. Up the steps came Roxie, a younger South African woman whom we had enjoyed on several other occasions because of her exuberant nature. She called out a greeting to us as she walked over, her long, curly red hair as alive as her smile. We listened to her latest tales with great enjoyment. We also talked about the politics of South Africa, plying Roxie with our questions. As we sat there, such a positive current of friendship flowed among us; I never thought about the fact we were only acquainted with these people for a week.

That night was the first of some very special evenings. The Dutch volunteers made dinner for us. What a treat. The pilgrims and volunteers sat together at long tables. We were seated with our newly found friends. The question naturally arose as to why we each decided to go on the Camino. We all shared our reasons, most of which were for spiritual or personal enrichment and growth. As we talked about some of the tough things about being a pilgrim, we sympathized and laughed a lot. I felt free and at home in the group. I went to bed that evening with a heart full of companionship and a stomach full of delicious Dutch food.

This sort of gathering developed a bond among us. We didn't know a lot about each other personally but we knew each of us had our ups and downs, our times of struggle and satisfaction. These shared experiences united us in our desire to be on the Camino. We had few expectations of continuing the friendships after we returned home, yet we knew we would be there for each other on the journey in any way possible. Our mutual experiences established a kinship between us that lent strength and care to our time together.

When the day came for us to say goodbye to the California couple I was unprepared for the emotion that arose in me. I did not want them to leave. They were the first pilgrim friends I bid farewell. The thought I would probably never have further communication with them left me feeling sad. I found comfort and enjoyment in their presence. Their departure signaled the first of many times when pilgrims I cared about moved ahead or stayed behind us.

GRADUALLY MY HEART ACCEPTED the temporariness of friendships that developed on the Camino. After Tony and Joan moved on, Tom and I discussed our feelings about their departure. We each felt the twinge of sadness in their leaving. We talked about how natural it is to resist investing in something not meant to last, in giving ourselves to a relationship we know is temporary. We reflected on how fewer and fewer neighbors know one another in our transitory and mobile society where people rapidly come and go. How much people miss by not reaching out and connecting with others even if it's a momentary relationship.

Out of this conversation, Tom and I coined the term "existential friendships" to describe the temporary relationships formed on the Camino. Unlike the philosophy of existentialism, we believed there was meaning and value in the short-term existence of our alliances with other pilgrims. These friendships contained purpose and worth for us even though they were short lived. They might exist for only a limited time but they merited an investment of our attention and care. We saw an example of this in our brief encounter with Tony and Joan. Even though the friendship would not carry over into the future, those two gave us companionship, understanding, and support—invaluable gifts for our spirits.

Not long after, some new friendships formed. Just when I thought we would not meet any other pilgrims we enjoyed as much as Tony and Joan, Marie and Aileen from England appeared on the scene the day we stopped to rest on the top of a high hill. Tom and I found a wooden bench in a government-sponsored herb and flower garden abandoned to scraggly weeds and overgrown grasses. As we sat there, two tall, thin women came up over the hill, waving to us. We recognized them from our brief stops in past villages but had not entered into any extended conversation. They paused to greet us and we talked a bit about the beautiful view from the high hill.

That was the beginning of another great friendship. Although I hesitated to reach out at first, still feeling the loss of Tony and Joan, I soon opened my heart to Marie and Aileen. It wasn't long before these two English women entered our ever-enlarging circle of friendship. In fact, Marie and Aileen continued to move in and out of our lives the rest of the way to Santiago. We reconnected with the two on our thirty-seventh day at the pilgrim Mass in St. James Cathedral. Later we sat with them at a little café, eating tiny stuffed peppers, sipping wine, and celebrating the end of the pilgrimage. Those two were such fun.

In the weeks to come after meeting Marie and Aileen, we got to know a variety of other pilgrims, among them were Karl from Switzerland, Nicolas from Austria, Helga and Marta from Germany, Rachel from Australia, Pierre and Michele from France, Elizabeth and Colette from New Zealand, and Philip from Canada. We were never without friends on the Camino. I had to trust this phenomenon each time one of them left the route or moved along at a faster pace than we did.

Occasionally we encountered pilgrims who were not in our lives long enough to term their presence a friendship but who left something of value with us that offered the quality of friendship. One such person was a tall, distinguished Belgian man in his fifties whom I mentioned earlier. We shared only one encounter, yet he left a definite mark on my Camino memory. We sat next to one another at an evening meal in Grañón and, although I do not recall his name, by the time we left the table I felt I had met him at a deeper level than some people I'd known for a lifetime.

The Belgian told me he and his wife had walked the Camino the year before and each experienced it as an amazing journey of spiritual growth. He decided to come back to walk the Camino alone while she cared for their eighteen-month-old granddaughter. This man longed to have solitude and time to go inward, "even further." What stays with me most of all was the man's response when I asked him about walking the mesa. His face and voice held a peaceful solemnity when he responded. The gentle pilgrim told us he liked the mesa, that it was a "good lonely" and assured us, with a knowing smile, that the mesa held surprises if we were open to it. He also told us he and his wife talked about things they never had discussed before when they walked the mesa.

Those words of wisdom helped when Tom and I were walking the mesa a week or so later. Because of that brief encounter of kinship, I felt at peace with the emptiness of the landscape and empowered to look for and find the mesa's hidden beauty. What I remember most about the Belgian, though, was his peace-filled spirit. His presence proved highly significant for me. Because of his keen perception and the obvious vitality of his spirituality, there was no doubt in my mind we could have been long-lasting friends if we met again beyond the Camino but even our momentary meeting that one evening blessed me.

THIS KIND OF EXPERIENCE brought the Camino to another level, one of greater depth and quality. The peace and joy that pilgrim friends bestowed in our brief times together awakened me to the value of existential friendships when I returned to my work.

Because I travel a lot to speak at conferences and retreats, I am constantly meeting and engaging with strangers for short periods. My time on the Camino encouraged me to invest more of my energy and presence in these transitory encounters because I now know the possibilities they hold. I no longer dismiss short periods of time spent with someone I may never see again because I know these brief encounters hold the seeds of existential friendship.

The camaraderie of pilgrims on the Camino encouraged me to be willing to invest more fully in something beautiful—even if it tends not to last for a long time. Those temporary friendships taught me that the simple existence of kinship can touch a heart and instill a lasting memory of goodness, a memory that inspires one long after the voice and the face are no longer remembered.

22

TRAVEL LIGHTLY

Every time each of us resists the urge to buy,
we are taking one small step to change our world.

—*Carol Christ*

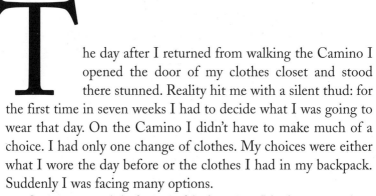

The day after I returned from walking the Camino I opened the door of my clothes closet and stood there stunned. Reality hit me with a silent thud: for the first time in seven weeks I had to decide what I was going to wear that day. On the Camino I didn't have to make much of a choice. I had only one change of clothes. My choices were either what I wore the day before or the clothes I had in my backpack. Suddenly I was facing many options.

Seeing so much before me felt daunting. I had grown to love traveling lightly on the Camino. Now I found myself returning to a complex world, one fraught with consumerism, with the pressure to look good and live a certain way to be socially acceptable. I did not want to return to this way of life. I longed for the simplicity the Camino had taught me. It was an uncomplicated way of living that I quickly realized was bound to be challenged each unfolding day of my return.

Traveling lightly is wonderfully freeing and essential for focusing adequately on what is within and around oneself. It does not, however, happen easily or all at once. It is a must for the pilgrimage to Santiago. Everything for the journey was carried on our backs. Many of the comforts of home needed to be left behind. No hair dryer, no electronics, no large fluffy towels, no bag of cosmetics. Just the basics, nothing more. In the months of preparation we learned what we ought to carry in our backpacks. It wasn't much. I couldn't imagine seven weeks without a little library of books. I found it hard to accept that I wouldn't have my portable CD player and a variety of CDs. Even selecting a journal challenged me. I knew I couldn't do without writing each day but my notebook would need to be a small one, not the usual thick 8½ by 11 inches.

A pilgrim has a minimal amount of "things" in their pack and every experienced pilgrim cautions it should not weigh more than 15 or 16 pounds. I promptly found out it doesn't take many items to total that amount. Tom bought a little scale and started weighing every single item he planned to take, even the smallest things like plastic bags, safety pins, a comb, a pen, mini-scissors. One day in late July he announced that he finally had his pack down to about 17 pounds. No matter how he tried, it was about the lightest he could achieve. That didn't sound very encouraging to me.

Then he loaned the scale to me and it was my turn. I found the process of weighing every item I hoped to put into my pack a test of my sanity. It was also a bit humbling. I thought I had a fairly simple lifestyle. I quickly found out this idea was a giant illusion. As the stack of items I hoped to take kept getting reduced, it turned out that I really had a lot of *stuff*. More and more things I thought would be helpful, or nice to have along, were put back in my closet, on the shelf, or into a chest of drawers.

As I was struggling with trying to keep the weight in my pack to a minimum, I came across an article in the daily newspaper about a forty-four-year-old father of two who was walking the length of Britain with only sunscreen, socks and the boots on his feet—"to celebrate the joys of nudity" he explained. I laughed and shared the article with friends saying: "Maybe I should travel the Camino this way. It would save me the frustration of weighing everything!"

Finally, after several weeks of annoyingly weighing every item, my backpack of seventeen pounds was ready. It contained these things which I considered essential and was unwilling to do without:

washcloth and a thin towel (12 by 24 inches)
2 thin socks for liners and 1 pair wool socks
tennis shoes (to give my feet a rest from boots at the end of
    the day's walk)
shower flip-flops
a pair of shorts and a knit top for sleepwear
short-sleeved tee shirt
shorts with zip-off pants
slim turtleneck and a stocking hat
lightweight wool cardigan
raincoat and pants
one change of underwear
two handkerchiefs
sleeping bag
vitamins, ibuprofen
hand lotion and sunscreen, basic toilet items (shampoo,
    toothpaste, and toothbrush . . .)
nail file clippers, small flashlight (an absolute must)
pocket knife, safety pins, needle, thread
small bar of soap (for washing clothes and shower)
foot stuff: moleskin, Vaseline, duct tape and an elastic
    knee-wrap
two bottles of water, 24 oz. each
small journal, pen, a very small book of Rabindranath Tagore's
    poetry
passport, small cloth purse, and money pouch
disposable camera

I wore lightweight pants, tee shirt, underwear, wide-brimmed
hat, sunglasses, hiking boots, wool socks, and sock liners. I carried
a water bottle in a holder at my side and my pack on my back.
Tom carried the maps, a tiny Spanish dictionary, and a small book
with Camino information on the route and refugios. We both had
a bit of food for lunch each day in our packs: a chunk of cheese, a

piece of fruit, a lump of bread, and sometimes nuts, raisins, or hard candy.

DESPITE ALL THIS CARE and caution to travel lightly, by the time we reached Burgos two weeks into our journey we paused to evaluate what we carried. Tom's tennis shoes were bulky in his pack and he was often irritated by their heaviness. He bought some lightweight sandals and sent his shoes home, along with my stocking cap, some hair conditioner, lotion, and several used disposable cameras. Not much but the load lightened a tiny bit.

Even one small additional item can impact how one travels lightly. On the day the elderly man gave me the huge tomato from his garden, I happily put it in my backpack's only available spot: the top flap. The rest of that day I couldn't understand why I was having so much trouble with wretched pain in my neck. I kept adjusting my pack but nothing seemed to work. At day's end when I took out the tomato I realized it had been heavy enough to pull my pack down on my neck. Imagine, a single tomato causing all that discomfort!

Since then I have observed how traveling lightly is not just about the amount of things we have, it is also how we allow those things to lead us away from what truly counts in daily life. These things tangle our attention and absorb our time, often creating more personal stress. They end up demanding way too much of our focus and energy—things like shopping for the right shade of lipstick or a certain piece of clothing; searching endlessly for the book we loaned and never got back and which we won't use but just want to be sure it's not lost forever; dusting a collection of little items that sit uselessly on shelves; or driving a great distance to a store that sells a brand name product.

Most everyone I know, including myself, has too many clothes, gadgets, knickknacks, books, music, you name it, yet we all spend an unbelievable amount of time shopping for more things to add to this collection of *stuff*. Then we use lots more energy taking care of it, being sure it doesn't get damaged, lost, or destroyed. This practice of having too much is often an unconscious way of distracting ourselves from what is happening at a deeper level of life. It deters us from entering into opportunities for greater meaning and fuller peace of mind and heart.

The Camino also taught me that traveling lightly is not just about having too many material things. Traveling lightly means divesting one's self of inner *stuff*, as well. This, too, can bog us down and keep us from being focused on what really matters in life. Emphasizing or being overly concerned about reputation, status, *looking good*, knowing enough, having an admirable social position can also deter us from walking on the road of life with a clear mind and a liberated heart.

Before Tom and I started out on the Camino we knew we needed to divest ourselves of most material things. We also wanted to rid ourselves of some of our *inner stuff*. This meant letting go of our personas. We both believed if we were known as a priest and a sister that people would keep us in those roles and not let us be our basic selves. We readily let go of our titles and were known as Tom and Joyce, good friends who were simply pilgrims on the way.

I also did not want anyone to know I was a published author. Staying in that role would keep me from traveling lightly. It would mean focusing on something other than the journey itself because pilgrims would not only treat me differently, I could also be distracted by their interest. Being quiet about this role was fairly easy, too. I longed to have an unencumbered Camino, to put aside what normally occupied my mind and heart. I knew if I could do this, then my inner self would be free and spacious enough to receive whatever lessons the Camino might offer me. I did not want my outer and inner *stuff* to crowd these lessons out.

What Tom and I discovered early on is that other pilgrims were of like mind. They, too, had stripped themselves of titles, personas, and roles that identified themselves as anything other than men and women walking the way to Santiago. Because we pilgrims rarely focused on our roles and our work back home, we were able to have conversations of great quality and worth that went beneath the surface issues of life. We did this without judging the other person because of their role or profession.

Rarely did anyone refer to themselves as someone other than a pilgrim but when they did, this usually happened only after they had become familiar to us. Two nurses revealed their professions when they helped to care for a severe case of blisters. Sometimes personal sharing required a revelation of work or home life such as a Frenchman in his fifties who sat with us at dinner one night. He had decided to walk the Camino in order to sort out his frustration and anger at losing his airline job of thirty years and chose to talk about it with us.

Several times I was tempted to move into my professional role. I longed to lead singing or to develop some creative evening prayer experiences for pilgrims at the refugios. As a retreat director, prayer and song are a treasured part of my ministry but I knew if I did this I would then be set apart and my Camino freedom might be limited. So I kept my retreat role to myself in an effort to walk freely and to be unencumbered by others' recognition and expectations.

WHILE I WANTED TO TRAVEL without the baggage of a religious role, I must admit there were times when it would have been very convenient to have used my title of Catholic *sister* to try for some pilgrim privileges. As a *sister* I might have been assured of a better bunk bed at a refugio or of some special attention as a counselor or a confidant. This never appealed to me, however, not even at my low point on the road when I was very ill and desperate for some physical comfort. The wonderful thing is that other pilgrims helped me out in my time of want, not because I was a *sister,* but because I was another human being who was weak and in need. I did not have to cling to my persona in order to be given the care

I required. They reached out because of their compassion and kindness, not because of my profession and role.

Traveling lightly stays with me now. The Camino convinced me I can live with less and be more satisfied. I regularly look around my living space and work area to view *all my stuff.* It is still way too much. Just like I weighed each item for my Camino pack, now I weigh mentally the things I want to purchase: Is it necessary? Is it worth the time and energy it takes to shop for it? Can I give something away of equal worth and measure? I also regularly weigh my inner stuff to see if it is too encumbering: How much focus am I giving to the expectations of others? When do I use my role to influence others? Am I working too much so that I neglect what is of most value in my life? Are there persistent thoughts and attitudes I need to discard?

These questions and decisions may seem tiny in the light of global decisions of justice and peace, or personal decisions like whether to continue chemo or get a divorce or have a child, but they are still vital decisions that affect my spiritual growth. The Camino taught me that traveling lightly will never be easy in a consumerist culture which emphasizes one's finances and importance. The Camino also taught me, however, that it is possible to be less consumed with stuff and more focused on the things that truly count.

MOST PILGRIMS STRUGGLED with the weight of their packs at one time or another on the Camino because it was so easy to try to have everything for the journey. There is a hilarious cartoon character painted on the side of a building along the Camino path. It depicts a pilgrim bent over with an enormous pack on his back. A large radio/tape player hangs from the curved handle of the staff he holds. All sorts of ridiculous items one ought never take on the Camino dangle from the bulging pack—an iron, a basket, an umbrella, a frying pan.

As I stood there laughing at that cartoon I also took careful note of how much it reflected my temptation to keep having more and more stuff in my life. When I keep gathering more things, they weigh me down as much as all those unnecessary items weighed down the pilgrim in that cartoon. The Camino convinced me that I only need to carry a certain amount in life's backpack. Having too many material things and too much inner clutter only burdens me and keeps me from being a truly free human being.

23

MATCH YOUR PACE TO YOUR WALKING PARTNER

Every relationship is a mixture of areas
where people meet
and areas where they do not meet
because the two people are different.

—*John Sanford*

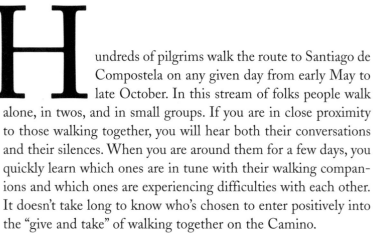

Hundreds of pilgrims walk the route to Santiago de Compostela on any given day from early May to late October. In this stream of folks people walk alone, in twos, and in small groups. If you are in close proximity to those walking together, you will hear both their conversations and their silences. When you are around them for a few days, you quickly learn which ones are in tune with their walking companions and which ones are experiencing difficulties with each other. It doesn't take long to know who's chosen to enter positively into the "give and take" of walking together on the Camino.

Because I chose to walk with a good friend of over twenty years, this daily attunement to the other person's physical, mental, and emotional pace was an essential ingredient of the Camino for me. Walking with another person yielded a terrific lesson. As a vowed, celibate woman of forty years, I thought I understood the challenges and blessings of my married friends but I learned a lot about the reciprocity of committed relationships while I walked the Camino with Tom. I must admit I returned with even greater admiration of anyone who strives day after day to balance their own needs and hopes with those of someone they live with and love.

Even though I lived with other members of my community in the past, I never constantly spent almost every part of a day with just one other person, certainly not for seven weeks. Tom and I discussed this aspect of walking the Camino before we left for Spain. We both were confident we would enjoy those weeks together. We had few doubts it would be anything but full of blessing for our relationship. In spite of this, Tom remarked a few weeks before we set out for the Camino: "I don't have any real fears but I do wonder if something could happen to create differences between us." I couldn't imagine this happening because we knew each other so well. It did get me thinking, however, that those many days and miles of walking would temper and shape how we related to one another.

Actually, I wasn't so much worried as I was intrigued about how our friendship would be influenced by the Camino. During the twenty years Tom and I had known one another our relationship had grown and deepened to the point where we called one another "soul friends." It seemed reasonable to expect that our extended time together would enhance and strengthen that friendship. Still, there was the nagging possibility he mentioned—perhaps being together for such an extended amount of time would hinder or even lessen the appreciation and love we had for one another.

There certainly is a risk in setting out on any great adventure with just one other person. After all, it is rather difficult to travel with someone for more than a week without some differences of opinion or some ornery mood swings temporarily influencing the tempo of the journey. After seven weeks of consistent presence with one another we were bound to encounter some irritations and annoyances.

Walking at the same physical pace proved the easy part. It was not that difficult to keep a steady pace with Tom as we crossed northern Spain. We moved at about the same tempo except when I got into my "hurry and push" mode. Because I normally tended to walk a bit faster than Tom, I walked a little way behind him on days when the path narrowed or when we went single file alongside heavily trafficked highways. Doing so allowed me to match his pace and not hurry him. This worked well for us even though a delightful feminist we met teased me about "walking behind my man."

OTHER PILGRIMS WALKING in twos sometimes had difficulty keeping the same physical pace. If one pilgrim had foot problems and needed to go slowly for a few days, this slowed the partner as well. When one person wanted to go on for more miles and the other one felt too tired, a mutual decision had to be reached. Tom and I met more than one couple who decided after the first week of walking to go separately for several weeks because of different physical stamina or an inability to get along with one another.

The Camino can bring out the best and the worst in a pilgrim. All sorts of things come rising to the surface in the continuous rhythm of walking. This obviously influences how two people get along. As in daily life, no one can plan for this ahead of time. There has to be openness to what might arise for both self and the other person. If the pilgrims are wise they will agree not to take it personally if the other person decides it is best to walk on alone. When I met Marie and Aileen they told me they were close friends for years. When they decided to walk together they promised each other that if they had any major disagreements on the Camino, they would leave it behind them once the pilgrimage was completed. They did have one week when they walked separately for several days but they said later it did not hinder their friendship because they wisely gave each other room to walk alone.

One pilgrim went on ahead of her companion because she didn't want to continually wait while her friend tended to her photography hobby. We also met Sarah, a young woman from the Midwest who was teaching English as a second language in Europe. She and her walking partner started out together but they soon agreed to go their own way. It was obvious from our conversation with Sarah that her friend was more interested in a newly found beau while Sarah wanted the solitude of the Camino, as she put it, "to work some things out."

Fortunately, neither Tom nor I were prone to moodiness or holding grudges. Our friendship was founded on mutual respect and kindness. We also shared a good balance between us in our temperaments: Tom's extroversion and my introversion. This balance proved to be a great gift for us on the Camino although Tom had queried beforehand in mock horror, "What do you think we'll talk about all day on those long walks?" He laughed but he was concerned. We had easily found many things to occupy our conversations while we trained for the Camino but the thought of days and days of actual walking on the pilgrimage seemed quite daunting to him.

I assured him in a joking way, "Oh, you can talk about the scenery, the other pilgrims, how much your feet hurt, and what kind of food you eat for every meal." We both chuckled but he raised a good point about how different we were in that regard. The last concern I had was what we would talk about. In fact, my introverted self relished the possibility of walking quietly and reflectively for long hours through lovely landscapes. I couldn't imagine myself talking all day long. Tom had a hard time imagining not talking.

As it turned out, we readily respected each other's need for conversation and quiet. I asked Tom if he would keep our first hour of walking in the morning for silent prayer. He ended up appreciating it as much as I did. In turn, I was grateful for our conversations during the day. This included mundane things but we also talked about what we were thinking and feeling. We drew each other's attention to beauty. We helped each other gain perspective when one of us was discouraged. We challenged one another when we spoke negatively about those we met on the way.

Our conversations were almost always effortless and natural. Neither of us felt overwhelmed by too much talk or too much silence. It was ironic that, as the days went on, I noticed how Tom grew more reserved as I grew more uninhibited. About three weeks into our walk, Tom said to me, "I think we've exchanged places. You are the one who's friendlier, reaching out to other pilgrims. I seem to be getting quieter." It was true. We couldn't figure out why it was happening but neither of us minded. It was another one of those Camino surprises, drawing out the undeveloped side of us.

There were times, though, when our emotional pace did not match the other's. When Tom felt exhausted by day's end and the guidebook maps were incorrect about distances or directions, he grew frustrated. On our sixth day coming into Estella, I was quite sure we had passed the refugio. Tom persisted in saying it had to be elsewhere because he was following the directions. We walked wearily for a good distance before we returned back to the place. It was the first time we had any significant irritation with one another on the Camino. It passed quickly but the moment was strong enough to serve as a warning that there could be other edgy differences in future days, and there were.

Inevitably, situations arose when we annoyed each other. Mostly, they were small exasperations. Tom's habit of talking to himself when he put everything back in his pack each morning started driving me slightly crazy. In the morning I heard him mumbling as he restored the items: "Okay, first the sleeping bag. There, good. Now, where did I put the extra pair of socks? Here they are. There goes the raincoat. Don't think I'll need it today. Where does this go? I wonder what I did with . . . ?" On and on went the monologue.

He did the same thing in the late afternoons when we settled into a refugio. He lay on the bottom bunk bed mapping out the next day's walk, reading the guidebook out loud, and talking to himself. I perched on the top bunk above him where I savored solitude while I journaled. After four days of this, I finally yelled down to him in a half-joking and half-serious tone: "Please, I don't need to know your every detail of life." Tom stretched his head out from under the bunk bed, looked up at me with a grin, and replied, "Why not?" He grinned some more and said, "Hey, I want to share *everything* that's happening in my life." He still continued to talk to himself out loud on future days but our little repartee kept it from developing into something that really rankled me. Being able to match our paces meant lightening up and not letting a situation develop into something more problematic.

We also differed occasionally on how much we wanted to walk and where. Like our climb to the castle in Villamayor de Monjardín, Tom felt excited and intrigued anytime an opportunity presented itself to climb up high and "get a good view." We came to one of these places in the region of Galicia. I felt bushed and it was only the middle of the day. The guidebook said the point was one of the highest on the Camino. It looked to be only a ten-minute steep climb but every step made a difference for my feet and legs. I testily resisted, "Do we really have to hike up there? We've already walked six miles and have at least six more to go. It's steep and full of brush. Let's just eat our lunch here on this rock."

Then I saw how much Tom wanted to go so I begrudgingly went with him. My walking companion was right in urging me to go. The sight was well worth the climb. We not only had a magnificent view but other pilgrims came and joined us. The little group of us experienced a delightful time as we sat high on the mountain eating our bread and cheese. Climbing the distance to be there on the mountain top eased my disgruntled mood, brought me joy, and helped me appreciate Tom's constant sense of adventure. I learned that day how entering into the *give and take* of companionship with another leads to unexpected happiness.

No huge factions or disagreements hurt our friendship but there were days when we talked more seriously about our misunderstandings and disappointments. The biggest obstacle concerned how much food to carry. As the weeks moved along, it seemed our backpacks weighed more and more. I hoped the longer we carried the packs the easier it would be. Just the opposite happened. Even carrying an extra piece of fruit was noticeable. Even so, I insisted on always having some food with us. My preoccupation with food was difficult for Tom. He began to balk at carrying food if there was a chance we could buy some along the way. It was always chancy to do this. Some days we didn't find anything so I would end up sharing my meager lunch with him. When that happened, neither of us had enough to eat and this irritated me.

We talked about "food." Tom agreed to carry some. The next day he took an orange, bread, and cheese in his pack. All morning long I heard him griping about the orange—how heavy it was, how he wished he didn't have it, how he couldn't wait for lunch so he could eat it. On and on he went about the orange. After two hours I turned to him and said, "Look, just eat the damn orange!" Tom was silent. As we went on walking, I slowly admitted I had spoken harshly to him. I turned and apologized for my remark. When we stopped for lunch at Rabanal del Camino Tom took the orange out, peeled and shared it with me. The orange tasted as sour as my words.

Another incident occurred a week or so later. At Eirexe two places were listed in the guidebook for food but when we arrived both of these were closed. As I stewed with frustration in the late afternoon, I wrote in my journal:

> *All in all, I am not happy with myself today. I should be able to go hungry, be in union with the homeless. Instead, I feel angry that we didn't plan better. I've stopped fighting about food, because Tom resists carrying it. I finally gave it up and didn't bother much about food today, and here we are, with barely enough for tonight. So I need to just "let go and let be." Yesterday Tom kept complaining about "how far yet to go" when he realized Portomarín was at the 94 km marker, not the 90 km. I told him he needed to "let it go" . . . and now it is my turn to stop and "let it go." He tried so hard to have this be a good place. He is such a kind person.*

We also learned that in trying to match our pace we sometimes tried too hard to please each other and then we both ended up being unhappy. There were two incidents within twenty-four hours that helped us become aware of this. We went for a short walk after the evening meal in Azofra and came upon a small park with a bench. We arrived at the time of sunset and the sky blazed with color. Everything in me wanted to remain seated and "be" with the beautiful scene. Soon, however, Tom arose to go. I didn't say anything. Instead, I walked back with him to the refugio, even though my heart longed to stay with the sunset.

The next day as we walked through Santo Domingo de la Calzada, a reverse situation took place. In the local church of this town a carved niche houses a rooster and a hen in commemoration of a miracle attributed to St. Dominic. I had no idea that Tom had his heart set on seeing this. As we approached the church, a Mass was taking place. No one was allowed to enter until it was over. We waited for some time but I got impatient and wanted to go on. Tom waited until we were out of town for about an hour and then expressed his disappointment at not staying and seeing the birds. I felt badly for him. We had a long conversation about how essential it was for each of us to make our needs known to one another. More importantly, both situations helped us see how we needed to "be with our self." Only when we chose to define our needs internally could we let the other person know what those needs and desires were. This awareness was vital in learning to match our pace.

The further we walked on the Camino, the more we grew comfortable with each other's internal pace. On days when Tom grouched about the distance left to walk, I encouraged him and cheered him on. I got him to sing Spanish songs with me or talk about good memories in order to ease his attention on his weary body. When my spirits sagged he did the same for me, getting me to lighten up and enjoy the journey.

One of the times he did this best happened when we walked from San Juan to Atapuerca in the great heat. We were both dog-tired as we came through a small forest of pines in the late afternoon. I grew grumpier and grumpier, grousing about the heat and the distance we walked since morning. All of a sudden Tom created a one-man morality play to help pass the time. It was hilarious. He had robbers coming out of the woods. "Ho! Who goes there?" says the knight guarding the queen in her coach. Tom went on and on until he came to a good moral ending where the queen pardons the knight for failing her and the knight goes directly to heaven. I laughed through it all and in no time we were through the woods and down the next two miles to the village where we found housing for the night.

MATCHING OUR PACES with each other enabled us to attune to one another's hearts. We talked about anything and everything. That was the best part. Not a day went by but what we reflected on how the day before went, how we presently were doing, and what we hoped for and feared about the road ahead of us. We easily and regularly expressed gratitude for one another's presence.

For some pilgrims walking alone is what they need for their growth. For me, walking with a trusted companion enhanced my own Camino gifts. Being a highly independent person, walking alone would only have reinforced my strong sense of independence and encouraged my introversion. It took but a few days for me to see the Camino was a lonely walk without a trusted companion. I needed someone to talk to about my growth-filled experiences.

Making the effort to match my pace to my walking partner proved well worth the gifts that came from it. The worth of this endeavor blesses anyone walking the path of life with another.

24

ENTER INTO THE HUM
OF HUMANITY

In the morning light, O God, may I glimpse again
your image deep within me, the threads of glory
woven into the fabric of every man and woman.
Again, may I catch sight of the mystery of the
human soul fashioned in your likeness, deeper than
knowing, more enduring than time.

—*J. Philip Newell*

The opening challenge on the Camino emerged when I lay down to sleep in the first refugio at Roncesvalles. I felt a bit anxious and wondered what it would be like to be in a situation for almost six weeks with little or no privacy, where many strangers slept in the same room I did, and where a lot of them would undoubtedly be snoring. That first night as I lay down in my bunk bed I was almost too tired to sleep. As soon as I quieted myself, I became aware of a phenomenal amount of noise.

All around me in the hundred or so bunk beds, I heard sleeping sounds. Men and women tossed and turned in their beds. As the woman above me rolled over, the side boards squeaked and her mattress rustled with the back and forth movements. Throughout the room there were sounds of wheezing, an occasional cough or the clearing of a throat, and snoring of all sorts: grunters, whistlers, snorters, locomotives, puffers, and wheezers. Some snoring was deep and resonant, others a steady whistle. This constant rhythm of heavy breathing filled the air. Weeks later I would jokingly describe this nightly symphony of sleep as "snoring in many languages." That particular evening, though, I wondered how I would ever endure many future weeks of such a cacophony.

As I lay there absorbing the noises, it occurred to me that listening to those varied sleeping sounds was a lot like listening to the steady *hum* in the woods I often heard on a summer's night back home. There, in my own comfortable place, I was enthralled and delighted with the evening lullabies of tree toads, frogs, crickets, locusts, owls, and numerous other creatures in the night woods.

Remembering this comforting experience, I thought, "This *refugio* with its many sleeping sounds is like the hum of summer, only here it is the hum of humanity. We are pilgrims from many countries. We represent the peoples of the world. We are all breathing together. Here in our beds we are simply human beings, vulnerable in our resting, having nothing to prove to one another. We are giving ourselves over to one of our most basic human needs: restorative sleep. This need unites us."

I felt a strong bond with my fellow pilgrims in that moment. The thought soothed me and I was able to go to sleep soon afterward. With rare exceptions, from then on I found it easier to rest within the vast array of sleeping noises. These sounds sometimes frustrated my own efforts at slumber but more often they cradled me with a consoling oneness that brought peace.

At various times after that first night I felt called to an awareness of the hum of humanity. I often felt myself a part of the Camino community and of humankind. This awareness came when I passed through villages and cities. In these places, I sensed a larger and diverse human presence as I mingled among the local people. Whether I was walking through the streets, stopping to eat, filling my water bottle at a fountain, or going into a store to buy supplies, I was briefly inserted into their life and activity.

Because of mingling among the mix of people, I was drawn out of my own small world and gifted with an entrance into theirs for a brief time. They were engaged in the same human activities as the people in my country were: buying and selling food, building houses, growing vegetables and grains, milking cows, taking children to school, talking on telephones, drinking in bars, driving cars. The facial features, the clothes they wore, and the language they spoke were different, but the deeper human traits were similar to my own.

ONE DAY, AS WE WERE coming down the Pyrenees, Tom and I stopped and took a break for lunch. While Tom napped on the pavement beside an old brick wall, I sat on some crumbling concrete steps across from a school playground. A small group of children about age ten or twelve were gathered in a circle playing cards under the shade of a large tree. Their chatter and laughter carried over to my heart. They were having a lot of fun.

Not far from the children, an elderly man also observed everything from where he sat on a pocked stone bench with his back against the brick wall. On the other side of me down the street one lone boy played with a soccer ball, kicking it against a wall. I knew none of these people. They were all involved in their own activities but with each one I felt a strong sense of relationship. We were all part of that hum, the resonant strain of humanness uniting us one to the other. Playing cards, sitting and resting, kicking a ball, all of these were common human activities.

This same sense of unity developed in me as I experienced other pilgrims. Because I was walking with just one other person, I had not considered that those who passed by us on the road or stayed at the same refugios might become a kind of community for me. Yet, that is exactly what happened. The strongest hum that vibrated in this community proved to be the bond of a common goal: walking the road. This bond came from the kinship of our going through a lot of the same challenges and struggles, the same joys and delights. This hum of humanity came from the blend of people from many countries being able to speak the same language of care and human kindness.

I was jolted into an awareness of this bond late one afternoon as I sat by an unsteady kitchen table in a small refugio. A dozen or so pilgrims were unpacking and milling around in the dormitory so I sought quiet and solitude next door where I could write in my journal. After about a half hour an Italian pilgrim in her early fifties entered the kitchen. We greeted one another and exchanged first names. Marianna then went over to the sink and chose a small tin tub from among the worn pots and pans. She proceeded to fill it with water and sat down to soak her sore foot in it.

As she sat down, I grew aware of my luxurious solitude in the last half hour and presumed she would probably want some time alone. I got up to leave, assuring her she could have use of the kitchen. She looked at me, put her hand up and objected, asking me not to go: "Please, please sit, please. Stay with me!" I thought she was merely being gracious but I sat down, anyway. Then, with struggling English she described her situation to me.

Marianna first told me about her sore foot. She was extremely worried about it, showing me where the pain was centered. I noticed that talking to me about her foot helped lessen her anxiety. It seemed to ease her concern somewhat. Fortunately, I knew one of the pilgrims staying there was a nurse so I went and asked her to give Marianna's foot some desired attention. The pilgrim-nurse assured her that the sore foot was not a serious medical problem and basically required some good rest.

That's not what Marianna needed most, however. This pilgrim needed human companionship, someone to talk to, about anything, it didn't matter. She was lonely. By the time I met her, she had been walking two weeks with her uncle. Marianna told me she had wanted to walk the Camino but could never find anyone to walk it with her. She didn't feel comfortable walking it alone. Her uncle found out and said he would walk the pilgrimage with her—even though he was eighty years old!

Actually, her old uncle was in excellent health and usually moved more swiftly on the path than Marianna. Age and agility were not the problem. The difficulty was that the uncle rarely spoke. The two had a respectful, caring relationship but he was a highly introverted man. Day after day they walked in almost total silence. To add to the loneliness, they had not met many Italians on the Camino. Because of the language difficulty and because both Marianna and her uncle were quite shy, they had little conversation with others. She longed for human contact, for someone to discuss the ups and downs of the Camino, to meet new friends and to enjoy meals together. By the time I met her, Marianna had swallowed her shyness in hopes she would finally have someone to talk to for awhile.

I introduced her to the other pilgrims in the refugio whom I had gotten to know. That began the start of a new Marianna. We met the two of them from time to time on future days and each time she appeared livelier and happier. Every time Marianna remarked how thrilled she was "to have found a sense of community on the Camino." It was another way of saying she had finally entered into the hum of humanity.

Marianna helped me see another way that each pilgrim on the road became part of an unseen bond. Hearing this lonely woman's story led me to understand how the strangers I met on the Camino desired a certain amount of solitude but also wanted engaging conversation. They were human beings with some of the same needs, wants, and hopes. Our common hum was not just in the physical pursuit and challenges of the walk. It was also in the mental and emotional needs and challenges. While the Camino vibrated with the feet of those upon it, the road also pulsated with the inner life of everyone who walked it. Each pilgrim formed a part of the long stretch of humanity that fed the community spirit on the Camino. I learned no one could or should be ignored or left out.

This became more and more apparent not just to me but to other pilgrims as well. The further we walked on the Camino the more open and hospitable all of us on the road became to one another. We grew in our awareness of how we were part of that *great hum.* It was most apparent at meal times. When a pilgrim was traveling alone, others would invite him or her to join in a cup of coffee or an evening meal, no matter if they spoke the same language or not. These meals were some of the most enjoyable times, when Spanish, English, German, Dutch, French, and

Italian blended into one table conversation. If one pilgrim knew a second language she or he would interpret for another pilgrim. At those times it mattered not what we had left behind or what our future held. There at the table we were pilgrims linked in spirit by our common experience of the Camino and the deeper joining of our humanity.

This affinity and communal bond became part of the day to day hum. When a pilgrim forgot a piece of clothing or some other precious item from their backpack, another traveler often carried it until he or she could connect with that pilgrim, like Carlos did for me. If someone had a blister and lacked the right medical applications there would be other pilgrims offering something from their packs to help out. The staff at refugios also gave advice and counsel about the road, the weather, and anything else that might help ease a pilgrim's walk a bit.

WALKING THE CAMINO would have been a very different journey for the two of us if we had not had the experience of the pilgrim community. Tom and I would have lacked the richness of personalities and diverse languages. We would have missed great stories and witnesses of courage, felt more alone in our struggles, and weakened by our challenges. Instead, the community of pilgrims enlivened our days and revitalized our verve. Our Camino days were always enriched because of their practical suggestions, insights, encouragement, joy, and laughter.

The Camino introduces pilgrims to a world of many faces and languages. This immersion into a vast array of foreigners can be exciting or threatening, depending on one's attitude toward the widely diverse community of companion travelers. One has a choice of either resisting whatever is contrary to one's own cultural comfort and personal ease, or moving into the unknown and the unusual with an openness to accept what one normally would not experience.

This is true for all people on our planet, no matter what life-path they travel. If we are aware and attuned to the larger community of humankind, we will gain strength and hope from our commonalities. If we look outward and allow our minds and hearts to stretch, every day we will be connected to the hum of humanity. As we walk the road of life we will find we are united at a deeper level with each person we meet.

Only on the surface do we experience differences. Beneath what seems to separate us as human beings are comparable hopes and numerous opportunities to enrich and encourage all. What a changed world it would be if the hum of humanity became loud enough to drown out the deafening roar of what separates and divides us.

25

PAUSE TO REFLECT

Your vision will become clear
only when you look into your heart.
Who looks outside, dreams.
Who looks inside, awakens.

—*C. G. Jung*

T he first time I remember deliberately turning around to look back and see the territory we had already walked was on our fifth day of the Camino. Tom and I walked steadily up to the Sierre del Perdón ("Mountain of Pardon"). At the highest point we stopped to take a breather at the intriguing memorial depicting the dream-filled Man of La Mancha standing amid life-size figures of Santiago pilgrims. Before we continued on the path leading steeply downward to the base of the mountain, Tom paused to look back. "What a great idea," I said, and turned around to join him.

The lovely city of Pamplona and the majestic Pyrenees revealed their beauty in the distance. Tom's voice filled with awe as he spoke: "Just think, we walked down those high mountains and through all that land. Can you believe we really did that?" I, too, was enthralled with the extent of what we already experienced. We stood there awhile longer, remarking about the beauty we beheld and the difficult slopes we managed to hike without any dangerous mishaps.

Although I was tired from the strenuous miles of previous days, a new burst of energy shot through me. I was amazed at how far we walked, how much beauty we received. The thought of other equally wonderful experiences on the miles ahead filled me with excitement. Even now I can sense the anticipation that arose in me as we turned away from where we traveled and continued to walk forward. Our brief pause to reflect infused me with renewed confidence and enthusiasm.

Our pause on the Sierre del Perdón gave us perspective. When we looked at where we previously walked, we saw the length, breadth, and height of it, something we could not fully comprehend when we were in the midst of it. Seeing this, we realized more fully what our bodies did for us in walking the many miles and we knew in a larger context the beauty our hearts received. This looking back served to reenergize us and give greater assurance that we could manage well what lay before us.

That first deliberate stop we took to look back and see the land we left behind us was the beginning of dozens of times when we paused to turn around. Almost every morning from then on, whether we left a tiny village or a large city, once we reached the outskirts or climbed a hill, one of us quietly stopped and looked back. This signaled the other to do the same. There we stood, sometimes in silence, sometimes quietly marveling at the beauty of the landscape or commenting on the conditions of the preceding day's route. Now and again, like the day we walked out of Azofra, we enjoyed gazing at a beautiful sunrise. Occasionally during the day, if we hiked a high path, we again paused to look back. Always this pausing on the Camino was a time of remembering and rejoicing as we looked at the miles we traversed, astonished at what the pilgrimage revealed. Each pause stirred an awareness of the wonder of our journey.

Our pausing to review where we traveled never seemed like an interruption to the pilgrimage or a clinging to the past. Rather, it was more a prayer of gratitude for the beauty of land and people, the gift of pilgrimage and the joy of companionship. We would have missed a lot had we not taken the time to look back on what we experienced. It was not enough to simply move forward on the Camino. We could not carelessly leave the past behind. The lesson of looking back convinced me that the best of the past influences the present and wants to be remembered.

C. G. Jung suggests "looking inside to awaken." Before leaving for the Camino I thought, "The outer world will be my source of awakening." I imagined learning a lot from the great outdoors as I constantly greeted new vistas and terrain. What I forgot is that the outer world remains a "dream" until it joins hands with the heart. Then it takes on deeper significance for our lives. Taking time to reflect on what has been, and is, draws these two significant spheres of outer and inner worlds together.

Besides turning around to view the physical world, Tom and I also turned around to look inside. We did this through deliberate reflective times such as writing in our journals. Tom's journal was tiny (3 by 4 inches) and mine a bit larger (6 by 9 inches). Neither was very thick due to the weight in our packs. I noticed that lots of pilgrims wrote in journals at the end of the day. Taking time to collect our day's observations enabled us to capture the sensual part of the day and bring it inside of us.

We also paused to deliberately reflect in the morning after we walked for an hour or so. At this time, we asked each other: "What part of yesterday was most significant for you?" Then we sifted and sorted through the past day's experience to see how it affected us. This sharing occurred as we moved along, without interrupting our walking pace. Our reflection was a great help because, as the weeks rolled along, I found myself mentally floating from one day to the next. The days might easily have become one big blur without the conscious focus we placed on what gave those days meaning.

THE PAUSES TO REFLECT wove our life experiences into a meaningful whole. They also helped acknowledge what went on inside of me, like the time I felt angry with myself and called myself "stupid" when I discovered I neglectfully left behind my Vaseline, duct tape, and moleskin for my feet. Of course, I didn't say any of this out loud. I just let it battle inside of me. The next morning when Tom suggested we ponder and name something significant from the past day, my inner funk came to the surface. After reflecting on it, I recognized what was happening to my spirit and why. This awareness eased my tension and drew me back into my need to lean on God and to forgive myself for making mistakes. Without pausing to reflect on my disappointing experience, my self-blame would have growled even louder inside of me.

Natural times of reflection also emerged when we paused with other pilgrims to join in conversation. Their questions and the ensuing dialogue provided another way of pondering the significance of the journey. As we responded to one another's queries, we each gathered emotional and spiritual pieces of our pilgrimage that might otherwise have been left behind. As others listened to me, I also listened to myself. I learned more of what it meant as I gave my reasons for choosing to walk the Camino, shared how the days were going, and discussed the challenges and blessings.

Throughout the Camino I valued reflection time but I never appreciated it as fully as when Tom and I reached the end of our pilgrimage. Neither of us thought about how we would reflect on and integrate the phenomenal experience of the Camino once it ended. We hoped for some extra days after arriving in Santiago so we could "relax and rest," but we never considered the possibility of taking extra days for reflection. As it turned out, we arrived in Santiago with five free days before flying home.

What a gift those days were for us! After consulting with a friendly travel agent named Paz, we took a two-hour bus ride to Finisterre, a lovely little town on the west coast. In Finisterre, we found inexpensive lodging. I couldn't believe our good fortune. Tom commented, "You know, we lead a charmed life. We found just what we needed at the Camino's end, like a rainbow's pot of gold."

The days we spent in Finisterre surprised and blessed us. During our last week of nearing Santiago, both of us had grown concerned about reentering the world we left behind in Iowa. We finally learned to walk in a relaxed manner and we feared losing this precious, newly found gift. Time in Finisterre offered the opportunity to ease our way from the unfettered life of the Camino to the hurried complexity of the world at home. As Tom and I sat in the living room facing a harbor of clear, turquoise water, we instinctively knew that the restful days immediately before us offered an opportune time to name where we had been and how we wanted to walk into the future.

From that first conversation in Finisterre we came up with eight questions:

1. What did we enjoy the most? The least?
2. What were the surprises?
3. Do we have any regrets?
4. What was most challenging?
5. What five key aspects of our pilgrimage do we want to share with others when we return home?
6. What are the central teachings and lessons of the Camino for us?
7. What do we want to integrate into our lives and how can we do this?
8. What are our concerns about reentry?

Those eight questions were marvelous springboards for our personal reflection. We discovered a splendid beach on the opposite side of the little town, just a twenty-minute walk from our condo. Each day we took two of the questions and spent the afternoons alone to ponder them on the beach. Tom enjoyed the almost deserted sandy seaside and spent most of his time there, sunning on the sand, dozing, and taking notes on the questions.

I found a cove with huge boulders where I relaxed, reflected, and wrote. The rhythm of the ocean's ebb and flow embraced my body and soul with welcomed rest during the long hours I spent pondering what the Camino taught me. The largess of the sea, so ageless, vast, and enduring, seemed the perfect place to pause for reflection. I felt both strength and comfort from the water. I, who had taken up residence on this planet in a world of water within my mother's womb, now reflected on another dimension of birth. The Camino's womb also nurtured profound growth. This priceless journey had stretched my sense of self while it strengthened my relationship with the divine and enriched my friendship with Tom.

When the two of us returned to our place on the harbor in the late afternoons we talked about what we gleaned during our beach-time reflection. (We did this, of course, while we were having a glass of good red wine!) We were heartened by one another's revelations as we shared from our quiet times. We found much similarity but also noticed things one or the other had either been unaware of or had forgotten.

During the first evening's conversation, Tom said, "I thought about the many little things that really helped our pilgrimage." He then went on and read his list: bunk beds by a wall to provide a tiny bit of privacy, ladders between the top and bottom bunks making the climb up and down easier, those little bits of shade on the mesa, soft grass cushioning our weary feet, village fountains to fill our water bottles, stones, logs, and benches on which we sat when we needed a rest. His naming of these things restored my gratitude for them.

As WE CONTINUED ON through the days of reflection and sharing, our responses to the questions expanded and deepened. Both of us grew astounded at our Camino experience. The list of teachings we discovered grew longer and longer. This book would never have been written had it not been for our reflection time in Finisterre, for it was there we first acknowledged and named most of the life lessons in this book.

Just as preparation for the Camino was as important as the journey itself, so, too, the reflection and integration time following it was vital. Without reflection on the Camino, my memories and insights might have slipped away. Without taking time to look back, much of what the pilgrimage provided for ongoing growth could easily have disappeared in the flurry of daily busyness.

Pausing and paying attention to where we have been helps us to learn more about ourselves and life by connecting our past to the present moment, by seeing how the past fits, or doesn't fit, with what we believe and how we live. Hanging onto the past is not healthy. Never looking back to the past is equally unhealthy. We need to look back in order to learn from where we have been, to carry these insights into the present, and to learn from them. When we do so we can walk into the future with greater wisdom.

I have thought often of pilgrims who told me they were going directly back to their own countries after arriving at Santiago. I cannot imagine how they did it without pausing for integration. I wonder if they took time when they arrived home to gather the teachings of the Camino for their lives. Did they review their journals? Did sharing with spouses, friends, and family serve to help the lessons thrive? Have the teachings they received from the Camino also stayed with them?

THE CAMINO REFRESHED my commitment to pause and reflect regularly. Webster's dictionary defines "pause" as "a short period of inaction." Pausing to reflect is my inner stop sign. In my hurried life, it is essential to "stop, look, and listen" before crossing to the next piece of life's journey. I need to deliberately ease up and be attentive to what is, as well as to what has been, in order to learn the lessons each piece of life holds. When I pause to reflect on my life events and experiences, I gain guidance, insight, and clarity. I reenter the territory of my life wiser and more grateful, reenergized for having connected the outer and inner aspects of myself into a meaningful unity. Each pondering and integration of life's pilgrimage prepares me for what is yet to come.

Since returning home, I have continued to pause and reflect on the richness of my Camino experience. Each time I do so, I gain renewed commitment to what I learned as I walked those many miles to Santiago. The ancient path's wisdom continues to inspire and challenge me every day. As I visit these teachings, they deepen in clarity and purpose. The Camino's lessons will continue to influence my life forever.

AFTER THE CAMINO

After our many weeks of walking the Camino, the day came when Tom and I stood on top of a hill and viewed the long-awaited city of Santiago. Tom cheered, "We're almost there!" Eager anticipation leapt up in me, too, but something else also moved steadily, catching me off guard. This "something" felt weighty. Gradually, a disturbing sense of sadness revealed itself. This emotion was confusing. "How can it be?" I thought. "I have waited for these final days, longed to complete the pilgrimage, but now that the time is actually here to end our walking, I sense a wall of resistance. A part of me wants to keep on going, to let the persistent movement take me forward into ever new vistas and discoveries."

Unknowingly, I had become attached to the steady pace of walking. No doubt about it—the pattern and motion of walking claimed me.

As we entered the city, I could hardly bear the thought of the Camino being finished. What a revelation to learn that my body had a mind of its own and this "mind" was demanding to keep up the rhythmic tempo. I assured myself the Camino would continue. The physical part was completed but the spiritual part, the joys and challenges of the pilgrimage, were only beginning to sink deep roots. This assurance did little to console me. The journey was ending. My body lamented having to let go and this lament entered my spirit. All I could do was coax myself into being less clinging. This coaxing took some doing but, after a few days, the sadness lessened as I readied myself to go home.

Little did I know, on my return, that walking would once again become vital for me. My body would be my soul's companion for inner healing. A time was coming when I would desperately need the solace and consolation of the steady movement of walking. This secret hid itself from me on that last day of the Camino but I glimpsed a hint of it during the following week of rest at Finisterre.

During one of those afternoons when I sat on the boulders by the sea, I looked down and noticed some grey, dried twigs at my feet. These small plants had sprung up between the large stones and later met their death either by salt water or in the turning of a season. Near the dead twigs, I also observed delicate flowers on tiny green plants. This fragile vegetation managed to sustain life while growing amid the cracks of weathered stones. As I observed the dichotomy of dried twigs and resilient green plants, an unexplained angst pulled at me.

I picked up one of the grey twigs. With the brown deadness in my hand, death grabbed my attention. "Go away," I snapped, wanting to avoid facing something so final. I much preferred focusing on the richness of the Camino with its beauty and bounty. I wanted to feel happy and contented. I did not like sorrow and melancholy surrounding me with their gauzy clutches but the gloomy mood anchored me with its power. I knew I had to listen.

There on the boulders I pondered life and death. I gazed at my sixty years, reviewed who I had become and wondered how I wanted to live out the rest of my days. The Camino would certainly influence my future. All those lessons along the way were too powerful to put aside. So were the difficulties I encountered. As I sat there, I felt badly about my response to the struggles. I wished I had been more of a "model" pilgrim with greater acceptance of what was tough. My impatience and my inability to accept the unwanted aspects of the Camino told me of my unfinishedness and my need for ongoing transformation. I said to myself, "I'd better 'get with it' before I die."

When I thought of how much growing I had yet to do, my mind turned to what I cherished in life and to the possibility of losing it through death. At one point in my reflection, I looked across the beach toward Tom who was relaxing in the sun. I thought of how dear he had become to me, of how much we had grown and deepened in our friendship during those many weeks as pilgrims on the road. He was an astounding witness to me of what it meant to be a kind, loving human being.

Tom's goodness encouraged my own. There on the rocks, seeing the little flowers amazingly alive in spite of their inadequate environment, I felt I could continue to be spiritually transformed in spite of what held me back. Greening plants amid dead ones called me to hope. I renewed my desire to be a more whole person, to accept the edges of my self that tried to rip apart my happiness. Before leaving the sea, a calm acceptance of my finiteness and my death took over my heart. At the same time, I also accepted the constant challenge of my "edges" and turned toward a desire to "let go" of whatever might be asked of me. I picked up my journal and wrote:

> *I've thought so much about death as I've watched the immensity of the sea this week. I realize that at my age of 60 I may not have lots of years left to live. I want to do my best, to live as lovingly as possible, to be as giving as I can of my gifts. Most of all, to be open to where and how God wants me to be. These promises I make before I turn my back on the splendor of the sea, the sand, the rocks, and the touch of the warm air upon me.*

It is perhaps best that we do not always know what awaits us, that we are unable to fully glean the messages that come from our intuition's nudges. What I did not understand that day of pondering mortality is that it was not about my death. It was about Tom's. The following April, just six months after walking the Camino, Tom died of a cerebral hemorrhage. Those precious weeks of living as a pilgrim on the way to Santiago were the spiritual preparation for his death.

As I look back now, I see that every step on the way to Santiago was a step that readied Tom for his ultimate pilgrimage home. The Camino was also a preparation for myself. His death was such a shock for me. All those lessons of the Camino that challenged me to "let go"—they were a source of strengthening me so I could let go of Tom when it was time.

After Tom's death, I continued to take daily walks even though it was excruciatingly painful not to have him beside me. Ironically, as much as the walking reminded me of Tom's absence, those regular treks also brought more comfort than anything else as I tended my loss. The steady rhythm of my body's movement kept my mind and heart in focus as nature cradled my sorrow. So many of the memories and lessons of the Camino returned to give me consolation. They softened the heartache as my feet and legs moved me along. Physically Tom was gone, but his laughter, advice, encouragement, and wisdom were always near.

Not long ago, I picked up my Camino journal and turned to the page from our last day at Finisterre. I had written in it on October 17th after I stored the items in my backpack in preparation for the bus ride to Santiago and the flight homeward. The demands, requirements, and responsibilities that awaited me at home stirred up some anxiety. During the night I awoke with a graced insight and wrote it down the next morning:

> *If my Divine Companion has guarded and guided me, kept me safe and healthy here, why would I not be taken care of when I return home as well? Yes, I need to trust . . . to gather all I've experienced, to grieve the end of the Camino, to be grateful for these relaxing days at Finisterre. And to let go . . . to walk into the future with courage, confidence, and a desire to serve with joy . . . to take the teachings of the Camino to heart, to integrate them into my life.*

Now the path leading to Santiago is far behind me. When I close my eyes I can see Tom and myself in that wonderful companionship on the road. We are walking the hills and valleys of the beautiful Camino. Then I open my eyes and see where I am—not on the Camino, but here. Alone. Yet, not alone. I am united with the community of pilgrims, with everyone who walks the continuing road of life with a sense of purpose and direction.

The Camino teaches the pilgrim to move on. One cannot stay

in the past. Like all pilgrims, I am meant to live in the Now, to continue to embrace the road of life as my great teacher. It is here that its lessons will sustain and strengthen me as I continue to walk in a relaxed manner. The Camino's gifts will endure just as love endures. Every pilgrim knows this.

NOTES

[1] *Camino* is the Spanish word for "road, journey, way, or path." There are a variety of caminos or walking routes in Spain. However, "the Camino" usually refers to the pilgrimage to Santiago which is described in Chapter 1.

[2] Doris Lora, "Edgar Mitchell, IONS' Visionary Founder, at age 73," Institute of Noetic Science, December 2003-February 2004, p. 19 (italics mine).

[3] Santiago (San Tiago) means *St. James.* The Camino de Santiago de Compostela is also known as the *Camino Frances,* the French Way.

[4] The complete text, *In the Name of All That Is,* can be found in the section marked Songs, p. 259.

[5] "Refugio" (ray-foo-ee-oh) is the Spanish word for refuge or shelter. Refugios are also called "albergues" along many parts of the Camino.

[6] All of the names of pilgrims have been changed in this book to protect their identities.

[7] These two symbols, the scallop shell and the yellow arrow, are directional markers for the entire route of the Camino.

[8] The literal translation of the Spanish word "mesa" is "table." Here it refers to a long, flat region of high, mostly treeless plains composed of pastureland and fields of grain.

[9] This is the famous Camino greeting given to pilgrims. It means "good walk" or "good journey."

[10] Most of the directors of the refugios were volunteers, sometimes referred to as "hospitalers" in reference to those who cared for ill pilgrims on the Camino during the Middle Ages.

[11] Rabindranath Tagore, *The Gitanjali,* #2, p. 24.

[12] Rabindranath Tagore, *The Gitanjali,* #18, #19, p. 37.

SONGS

The following songs lifted our hearts on the Camino as we sang them each morning while we walked along.

In the Name of All That Is

In the name of all that is, we come together.
In the name of the stars and galaxies,
In the name of the planets, moons, and the stars,
In the name of all that is, we come.

In the name of all that is, we come together.
In the name of the ocean and the sea,
In the name of the mountain, desert, and plain,
In the name of all that is, we come.

In the name of all that is, we come together.
In the name of the buffalo and bear,
In the name of the turtle, eagle, and whale,
In the name of all that is, we come.

In the name of all that is, we come together.
In the name of the cactus and the fir,
In the name of the flower, tree, and the earth,
In the name of all that is, we come.

In the name of all that is, we come together.
In the name of the elements of life,
In the name of the soil, water, and air,
In the name of all that is, we come.

In the name of all that is, we come together.
In the name of the children of the Earth,
In the name of the Spirit breathing in all things,
In the name of all that is, we come.

In the name of the Spirit breathing in all things,
In the name of all that is, we come.

From the CD: *In the Name of All That Is.* Available from: Jan Novotka, 421 17th Ave., Scranton, PA 18504. 570-347-2431. www.jannovotka.com

Vienen con Alegría

Vienen con *alegría,* Señor, cantando vienen con *alegría,* Señor,
los que caminan por la vida, Señor, sembrando tu paz y amor.

1. Vienen trayendo la esperanza a un mundo cargado de ansiedad,
   a un mundo que busca y que no alcanza caminos de amor y de
   amistad.

2. Vienen trayendo entre sus manos esfuerzos de hermanos por la paz,
   deseos de un mundo más humano que nacen del bien y la verdad.

3. Cuando el odio y la violencia aniden en nuestro corazón,
   el mundo sabrá que por herencia le aguardan tristezas y dolor.

They Come with Joy

They come with joy, Lord, singing, they come with joy, Lord,
Those who walk through life, Lord, sowing your peace and love.

1. They come bringing hope to a world heavy with anxiety,
   to a world that seeks and cannot reach the roads of love and
   friendship.

2. They come bringing in their hands efforts for peace among all,
   desires of a more human world that births goodness and truth.

3. When hate and violence fill our heart,
   the world will know that by inheritance sadness and hurt are
   expected.

Alabaré

Alabaré, alabaré, alabaré a mi Señor.
Alabaré, alabaré, alabaré a mi Señor.

1. Juan vio el número de los redimidos,
   y todos alababan al Señor;
   unos oraban, otros cantaban,
   y todos alababan al Señor.

2. Somos tus hijos, Dios Padre eterno,
   tú nos has creado por amor;
   te adoramos, te bendecimos,
   y todos cantamos en tu honor.

3. Todos unidos, alegres cantamos
   gloria y alabanzas al Señor.
   Gloria al Padre, gloria al Hijo,
   gloria al Espíritu de amor.

I Will Praise

I will praise, I will praise, I will praise my Lord.
I will praise, I will praise, I will praise my Lord.

1. John saw the number of the redeemed,
   and all praised the Lord;
   some prayed, others sang,
   and all praised the Lord.

2. We are your children, Father God eternal,
   you have created us in love;
   we praise you, we bless you,
   and all sing in your honor.

3. All united, we sing happily
   glory and praises to the Lord.
   Glory to the Father, glory to the Son,
   and glory to the Spirit of Love.

Juntos Como Hermanos

Juntos como hermanos, miembros de una Iglesia,
Vamos caminando al encuentro del Señor.

1. Un largo caminar, por el desierto bajo el sol.
   No podemos avanzar sin la ayuda del Señor.

2. Unidos al rezar, unidos en una canción,
   viviremos nuestra fe con la ayuda del Señor.

3. La Iglesia en marcha está. A un mundo neuvo vamos ya
   donde reinará el amor, donde reinará la paz.

Together as Brothers (and Sisters)

Together as brothers (and sisters) members of one church
let us go walking to meet the Lord.

1. It is a long journey through the desert under the sun.
   We cannot move forward without the help of the Lord.

2. Together in prayer, together in song,
   we will live our faith with the help of the Lord.

3. The church is marching toward a new world
   where love will reign, where peace will reign.

Test and arrangement © 1979, Cesáreo Gabaráin. Published by OCP Publications, 5536
NE Hassalo, Portland, OR 97213. All rights reserved. Used with permission.

SOURCES RELATED TO PILGRIMAGE AND THE CAMINO DE SANTIAGO DE COMPOSTELA

The Camino: A Journey of the Spirit, Shirley MacLaine
El Camino: Walking to Santiago de Compostela, Lee Hoinacki
My Father, My Daughter: Pilgrims on the Road to Santiago, Donald Schell and Maria Schell
Following the Milky Way: A Pilgrimage on the Camino de Santiago, Elyn Aviva
Fumbling: A Pilgrimage Tale of Love, Grief, and Spiritual Renewal on the Camino de Santiago, Kerry Egan
Off the Road: A Modern-Day Walk Down the Pilgrim's Route into Spain, Jack Hitt
On Pilgrimage: Sacred Journeys around the World, Jennifer Westwood
On the Road to Santiago, Bob Tuggle
Peregrina: A Woman's Journey on the Camino, Marilyn Melville
The Pilgrimage to Compostela in the Middle Ages: A Book of Essays, edited by Linda Kay Davidson and Maryjane Dunn
The Pilgrim's Guide to Santiago de Compostela, William Melczer
The Pilgrimage, Paulo Coelho
The Pilgrimage to Santiago, Edwin Mullins
The Pilgrimage Road to Santiago: The Complete Cultural Handbook, David M. Gitlitz and Linda Davidson
Pilgrim Stories on and off the Road to Santiago, Nancy Louise Frey
Pilgrimage to the End of the World : The Road to Santiago de Compostela, Conrad Rudolph
Roads to Santiago, Cees Nooteboom
Sacred Places, Pilgrim Paths: An Anthology of Pilgrimage, Martin Robinson
The Singular Pilgrim: Travels on Sacred Ground, Rosemary Mahoney
Walking the Camino de Santiago, Bethan Davies

The Pilgrim Cards

These beautiful reflections provide a source of tapping into one's own inner wisdom. The creator of these cards, Austin Repath, has walked El Camino de Santiago three times. During these pilgrimages, he began mapping the inner landscape of the soul as it traverses the joyful heights and dark valleys of the human journey. Available through http://www.pilgrimcards.com or at 252 Salem Ave Toronto ON M6H 3C7 Canada.

These two guidebooks (and maps) were our lifelines when we walked the Camino

Pilgrim Guides to Spain: The Camino Francés (St. Jean-Pied-de-Port to Santiago de Compostela), David Wesson. The Confraternity of St. James, 27 Blackfriars Rd., London SE18NY. editorc@csj.org.uk (This guidebook is regularly updated. Contains information on the refugios on the Camino de Santiago de Compostela.)

A Practical Guide for Pilgrims: The Road to Santiago, Millán Bravo Lozano. Editorial Everest, S.A., 2002. (Comprehensive information on historical and cultural interests on the Camino, details of the route itself, as well as listings of most housing available along the way. Excellent set of detailed maps.)

Central Organization for the Camino de Santiago de Compostela (also called: El Camino Francés)

The Confraternity of St. James is the most helpful organization for walking the Camino. They publish maps and guidebooks. The pilgrim passport can be secured through this organization (or at one of the refugios on the Camino).
www.csj.org.uk
office@csj.org.uk
27 Blackfriars Rd.
London SE1 8NY
UK
Tel: (+44) (0) 20 7928 9988
Fax: (+44) (0) 20 7928 2844

Useful Websites

http://www.americanpilgrims.com
www.caminosantiagocompostela.com
http://www.backpack45.com/camino2p2.html
http://www.santiago-today.com/
www.kitsjourney.com.
www.caminovideo.com.
www.peterrobins.co.uk/camino/Caminos.html